"As a parent of three children with SEND, I would have loved to have a book like this when we began navigating our own journey of SEND support and EHCPs in school. *The SEND Handbook for Parents and Carers* is a really useful guide which helps to outline SEND systems and the support available in schools whilst explaining key terms used. With helpful ideas and tips, this book is a must-read for parents who are supporting a school-aged child with SEND." – **Tamsin Grimmer**, *Early Years Consultant and parent of three autistic girls*

"This book works through the rollercoaster ride that is SEND parenting in such a clear, simple way and is easy to read and return to at different stages of your parenting journey [...]. Every parent of a child navigating the SEND pathway in education should have a copy of this book." – **Cheryl Warren**, *SEND Trainer and Consultant; Director, Aperion Training*

"This book is an invaluable resource to help parents navigate the SEND system. I wish I had had a copy when going for my child's Education, Health and Care Plan, EHCP; it could have saved us time and stress!" – **Alice Hoyle**, *Wellbeing Education Consultant and mum of three*

THE SEND HANDBOOK
for Parents and Carers

Being a parent of a neurodivergent child can be challenging and exhausting. It can feel like a constant battle to be heard and to gain the support that you and your child need. This book provides an accessible overview of the SEND system and how it works, so that you can successfully untangle and navigate the system and draw upon the best resources offered.

The handbook is divided into three main parts: SEND systems, policy and legislation; support for your child in school; and looking forward. Chapters:

- Introduce the world of SEND systems and break down key documentation and the roles and responsibilities of school staff.
- Take you on your child's journey through school and explore key aspects from assessment and EHCPs, to funding and gaining further support for your child.
- Look ahead and consider important transitions through each of the school phases in your child's journey and allows you to acknowledge some of your own fears and challenges as a parent.
- Include a range of both practical and reflective activities to bring each area to life.

The voices of parents and carers are woven in throughout the book, as well as key staff who you might encounter, from occupational therapists to speech and language therapists. This comprehensive guide will be an essential tool to support your journey to get the best from your child's school experience.

Sarah Alix has worked in education for nearly 20 years, with experience across a range of settings including schools and universities. She has a Doctorate in Education, a psychology degree, and post-graduate qualifications including the SENCo award and PGCert in Autism. Sarah currently works for the Sigma Trust in Essex leading the teacher training provision and is a Senior Fellow of the Higher Education Academy. She has a great personal awareness and understanding of neurodiversity through her own family members.

THE SEND HANDBOOK

for Parents and Carers

How to Navigate the SEND System and
Support Your Child Through School

Sarah Alix

Routledge
Taylor & Francis Group

LONDON AND NEW YORK

Designed cover image: © Getty Images

First published 2025
by Routledge
4 Park Square, Milton Park, Abingdon, Oxon OX14 4RN

and by Routledge
605 Third Avenue, New York, NY 10158

Routledge is an imprint of the Taylor & Francis Group, an informa business

British Library Cataloguing-in-Publication Data
A catalogue record for this book is available from the British Library

ISBN: 978-1-032-68912-8 (hbk)
ISBN: 978-1-032-68910-4 (pbk)
ISBN: 978-1-032-68915-9 (ebk)

DOI: 10.4324/9781032689159

Typeset in Caslon
by Deanta Global Publishing Services, Chennai, India

CONTENTS

About the Author   ix

Acknowledgements   xi

Introduction: How to use this book   xiii

PART I
SEND SYSTEMS, POLICY AND LEGISLATION

CHAPTER 1   3
How Did We Get Our Current SEND System in Schools?

CHAPTER 2   19
What Is the Code of Practice and What Does it Mean? The Roles and Responsibilities of School Staff

PART II
SUPPORT FOR YOUR CHILD IN SCHOOL

CHAPTER 3   39
How Your Child is Assessed in School: The Graduated Approach

CHAPTER 4   57
Education, Health and Care Plans: What Are They, How to Apply and How to Appeal a Decision

CHAPTER 5   75
Funding and Support for Your Child

PART III
LOOKING FORWARD

CHAPTER 6   93
Transitions: From Early Years to Post-16 and Beyond

CONTENTS

CHAPTER 7   107
How to Get the Most from Parents' Evenings, Review Meetings and
Annual Reviews

CHAPTER 8   119
Supporting Your Child at Home with Their Education

CHAPTER 9   131
What Next for Your Child?: Looking to the Future

Glossary of Key Terms   135

Index   137

ABOUT THE AUTHOR

Sarah Alix has worked in education for nearly 20 years. She works for the Sigma Trust in Essex leading the teacher training provision. Sarah has experience as a youth worker, a primary school teacher, a behaviour support adviser working with primary, secondary and special schools, and working for a university as a Senior Lecturer and Deputy Head of their Education Department.

Sarah has a Doctorate in Education, a psychology degree, and many post-graduate qualifications including the SENCo award, PGCert in Autism, MA in Education, and PGCert in HE. Recent publications include The Neurodiversity Handbook for Trainee Teachers, The Neurodiversity Handbook for Teaching Assistants and Learning Support Assistants, The SEND Handbook for Primary Trainee Teachers, and a handbook for foster carers. She is a school Governor across multiple schools, and enjoys a focus on supporting SEND development in schools.

Sarah is also a Senior Fellow of the Higher Education Academy, a graduate member of the British Psychological Society and a Fellow of the Chartered College. She is part of the Autism Education Trust Expert Reference Group and Schools Reference Group.

Sarah has a great personal awareness and understanding of neurodiversity through her own family members who are autistic, have attention deficit hyperactivity disorder, dyslexia and general anxiety disorder, and through her own diagnosis of autism as an adult a few years ago. She understands the challenges of being a parent and trying to understand how to support your child in the best way as they progress through school with SEN.

Sarah has a strong belief that this is where it all starts; education, and that the school years lay the foundation for everything else to come, whether this is to work in health, finance, the arts, business or education to name a few, it all starts with the building blocks of school. This is why it is so important to understand how you can support your child through working with schools in collaboration.

Alix, S. (2023). The Neurodiversity Handbook for Trainee Teachers. SAGE Publications.

Alix, S. (2023). The Neurodiversity Handbook for Teaching Assistants and Learning Support Assistants; A Guide for Learning Support Staff, SENCos and Students. Taylor and Francis.

Alix, S. (2024). The SEND Handbook for Primary Trainee Teachers. SAGE Publications.

Alix, S. (2020). The Foster Carer's Handbook on Education; Getting the Best for Your Child. CoramBAAF.

ACKNOWLEDGEMENTS

After writing several publications on neurodiversity and SEND for school staff, I thought that it was really important to write a book to support parents and carers. I know how difficult it has been for myself as a parent supporting my own children through education, and I now draw upon my own knowledge, understanding and networks in education to write this book. I would like to thank editor, Clare Ashworth, and editorial assistant, Molly Kavanagh, for their valuable support and guidance along the way. I would like to thank my reviewers for their valuable and supportive feedback. I would also like to thank each of my children; Charlie, Morgan and Maximilian for being the unique individuals that they are. It is important to thank everyone that has supported and helped me to write this book, given me insight, and have had discussions with me to form the case studies.

INTRODUCTION

HOW TO USE THIS BOOK

This is a practical support book for parents and carers to understand the SEND systems in school, and ways in which to support their child as they progress through the schooling system.

The chapters move through key areas to support your child; looking at the SEND system that is in place, and policy and legislation that underpins it; ways in which your child is supported in school and how they are assessed; and looking forward at transition points, how to get the most from parents' evening and review meetings, and what you can do next for your child.

The chapters draw upon expertise from Lead SENCos in schools across the age phases, Teachers, and most importantly, personal experiences from a range of parents and carers of supporting their children.

The book contains five types of interactive features throughout:

1. **Reflect** opportunities for the reader to reflect and think of questions or about questions
2. **Professional Discussion** for the reader to have with their child's class teacher or SENCo
3. **Activity** opportunities to find something out or seek further information
4. **Case Studies** demonstrating examples of practice for reflection or discussion
5. **Top Tips** to think about or to use

FACING YOUR FEARS AS A PARENT

Being a parent of a child with SEND can be difficult, and I understand this from my own personal experience as well as from working as an educational professional. You have probably already had many struggles yourself if you are reading this book. It might be from deciding if your child may have additional needs, trying to work with a school to find the best strategies to support them, or feel as though you are fighting a system to get the support that you need for your child. The two case studies below are an introduction to the book and are from parents outlining their own difficulties in processing their child's needs.

CASE STUDY

From a Parent Receiving a Diagnosis for Their Child

When Cameron was young, I didn't expect that anything was different. He was a boy, different to my daughter and how she played, but I just put that down to him being a boy and I didn't have any experience of bringing up boys. At nursery, he had some speech difficulties and received speech and language therapy which went well. He then progressed to primary school, and this is when his teachers started to say to me that they had some concerns. They thought that Cameron was over-emotional, and there were some things that were just not clicking into place for him. He was referred to a paediatrician, and then for an autism assessment. I started reading up on autism, and sometimes I would think that I could see this in him, and other times, I thought he looked just like every other 7-year-old child. I read up about lots of different conditions, including auditory processing disorder as I thought he may have difficulty processing things, and sensory challenges.

I stayed in for the assessment, and I could see how Cameron was reacting to some of the activities. For example, they showed him a puzzle and asked what he could imagine in it, he said triangles and squares, the assessors gave him prompts and asked could he see a kite or a plane for example, but each time he just said triangles.

When I attended the appointment to get the results of Cameron's assessment, I tried to prepare myself that he wasn't autistic, and kept thinking, well, what's next? Is he having difficulty because of something else? I therefore didn't prepare myself for a diagnosis that it was autism.

I remember sitting in the room and the doctor saying that he had clearly met the criteria for autism. I wasn't sure if I was relieved that I knew why he was struggling and therefore could work out what to do next, or shocked because I hadn't prepared myself for a diagnosis.

I left the room and returned Cameron to school, and as I drove away, I cried and cried. I had to pull over. I kept thinking but what next, what will life be like for him, will he ever be independent, will he have friends. I felt so overwhelmed, and didn't know how to talk to anyone about it. I felt as though I was in some way grieving for a child he was never going to be. I watched a group of boys walking past, chatting and being silly, and I thought, Cameron may never be like that.

It was quite a shock at the time, and it took me quite a long time to process what this would mean for Cameron. Years on, although I still worry about what life for Cameron will be like and how he will need support, there are a lot of things now falling into place as he is getting older. For example, Cameron now has a small group of close friends. He plays gaming with them, and he goes out (with an adult keeping an eye on them) to go Pokémon hunting. He is acting like a normal teenager in many ways, and although he has a lot of difficulties and challenges, he is a kind and wonderful young man and I am very proud of how far he has come.

CASE STUDY

From a Parent Receiving Their EHC Draft Plan for Their Child

Applying for an EHC plan for Keisha had been a long and difficult journey. Keisha had been struggling at school for a number of years. The school had gathered a great deal of evidence, including IEPs, reports from support workers and an Educational Psychologist report. We had been asked for our own views too, and for Keisha's views, and we contributed to the assessment.

When I received the draft EHC plan, I sat and read it through cover to cover. I remember stopping part way and taking a deep breath, it was tough to read. It was like gathering all your concerns and child's problems and condensing them into one report, all their struggles and challenges, everything that Keisha couldn't do. It was such hard read and it brought tears to my eyes. My husband came in and I gave him the copy to read through, I can still see the picture in my mind of him sitting on the sofa, and the big sigh that he gave as he took a break before carrying on with reading it. It was quite hard hitting. I know that it needed to contain all the detail, and my husband and I sat in silence for a while. Keisha then walked in, a big smile on her face telling us that she had just managed to zip her own hoodie up, and that meant she would now like to go to the park as she was dressed right! We all laughed and I thought about how much she *could* do. The report was demonstrating what was needed which would inform her support, but Keisha is more than a report, and although this is useful to inform support for her, we focus on all the things that she can do, and how we build on these.

Some of you will be just starting your SEND parenting journey, and other readers will have already faced years of working hard to get things right and in place for your child. Parenting a child with SEND can be really challenging. It can be stressful, emotional and demanding. But your child also brings a great deal of joy into your life, and the fight to give them the best that you can will continue throughout their lives. I hope that this book will provide some guidance and advice for you along the way to support your child.

KEY DOCUMENTS THAT ARE REFERENCED THROUGHOUT THIS BOOK

The Code of Practice (CoP)

The Special Education Needs and Disabilities (SEND) Code of Practice (CoP) 2015: This is a statutory code which contains the legal requirements for Local Authorities and schools. It outlines the roles and responsibilities that everyone has in relation to supporting pupils with SEND.

The SEND and Alternative Provision (AP) Improvement Plan

This very recent plan sets out the government's proposals to improve outcomes for pupils through:

✦ Improving experiences for families, reducing the current adversity and frustration that they face.
✦ Deliver financial sustainability of the system.
✦ Relieve pressure on the current AP sector.

REFLECT

Consider where you are on your SEND journey with your own child, are you new to being a SEND parent with a child in school, or are you an experienced parent that has dealt with challenges and choices for their child and their education?

This book aims to give some guidance to both new SEND parents and experienced SEND parents, it can be read cover to cover, you can dip into chapters as you need them, or use it to refer back to or to give you support, skills and information when you need them.

PART I

SEND SYSTEMS, POLICY AND LEGISLATION

REFLECT

Consider where you are on your SEND journey with your own child, are you new to being a SEND parent with a child in school, or are you an experienced parent that has dealt with challenges and choices for their child and their education?

This book aims to give some guidance to both new SEND parents and experienced SEND parents, it can be read cover to cover, you can dip into chapters as you need them, or use it to refer back to or to give you support, skills and information when you need them.

DOI: 10.4324/9781032689159-1

HOW DID WE GET OUR CURRENT SEND SYSTEM IN SCHOOLS?

CHAPTER AIMS

- ✦ To give an overview of how policy and legislation relating to SEND has brought us to what is in place in schools now.
- ✦ To outline the Local Authority's (LA) role in providing provision for SEND pupils.
- ✦ To introduce the Code of Practice (CoP) and how this is implemented within schools.
- ✦ To introduce the changes to SEND practice in schools.
- ✦ To give a meaning of inclusion and the different educational settings for SEND pupils.
- ✦ To explore the meaning of intersectionality, and consider the possible impact for your own child.

INTRODUCTION

This first chapter is going to give you an overview of the policy and legislation in place for SEND pupils. It will give you an understanding of the bigger picture, setting the context, of what happens within politics that directly affects your child in school.

Throughout the book, I will refer to 'child' and 'pupil', and the terms will be used interchangeably. When referring to your perspective, I will refer to your 'child' and when referring to the perspective of a school, I will refer to their 'pupil' for the majority of the time, however, at times it may be difficult to clarify the perspective as it will be both, and therefore either term may be used.

The Local Authority (LA) has a direct responsibility for providing provision for your child, and this will be looked at here too. Their role is looked at in more detail in Chapter 5 when we explore Education, Health and Care Plans (EHC plans/EHCPs).

DOI: 10.4324/9781032689159-2

What Is a Special Educational Need or Disability? The Definitions of SEND

If a child has a Special Educational Need or Disability, they may need to have a different or additional provision made for them. The Department for Education (DfE) (2015) outlines this as:

◈ If there is a significantly greater difficulty in learning than the majority of others of the same age, or

◈ If they have a disability which prevents or hinders them from making use of facilities of a kind generally provided for others of the same age in mainstream schools or mainstream post-16 institutions.

(DfE, 2015)

You may have heard of 'The Equality Act' which is a law that protects people from discrimination. Discrimination is the unfair treatment on the basis of certain characteristics, known as 'protected characteristics' and they include age, disability, being married or in a civil partnership, being pregnant or on maternity leave, gender reassignment, sex, sexual orientation, race, nationality, ethnic or national origin and religion or belief. The purpose of the Equality Act is to ensure a fair and equal society.

The Equality Act (2010) states that a child who has Special Educational Needs (SEN) may have a disability if they have a 'physical or mental impairment which has a long-term and substantial adverse effect on their ability to carry out normal day-to-day activities'. Long-term is defined as a year or more, and substantial meaning more than minor. Children with impairments such as a sight or hearing loss, or a long-term health condition such as diabetes, epilepsy or asthma are within this category. However, children such as with these conditions do not necessarily have Special Educational Needs but there can often be an overlap of needs and children with conditions such as these.

How Policy and Legislation Has Developed

The first defining moment for Special Educational Needs pupils in schools was when SEND was categorised as a disability and introduced within the Education Act 1944, with pupils being placed within special schools. Thinking around SEND moved on over the next few decades, and in 1981 a more integrated approach to provision and inclusion was considered.

A key document was introduced outlining the duties of the school, the Special Educational Needs Co-ordinator (SENCo) and teachers is the Code of Practice (CoP) (2015). The CoP has defined what practice in schools looks like for the last decade. The Department for Education (DfE) (2015) sets out their vision for SEND within this document for pupils with SEND which

is the same as for all children and young people – that they achieve well in their early years, at school and in college, and lead happy and fulfilled lives.

(DfE, 2015).

However, change is imminent for schools and pupils. There have been recent consultations on SEND to be incorporated with the new schools' legislation white paper (2023). From this the government has drawn up a SEND and Alternative Provision (AP) Improvement Plan. It will take many years for this to be implemented and change will be slow, but keeping on top of what this looks like for your child in school will be important so that you know and understand what to expect for your own child and when, as things will change and develop over the next decade.

It is always important to note that with changing governments, all politicians want to bring in their own ideas and changes, and again, at any time, this can take a turn and go in another direction.

Table 1.1 outlines the key policy and legislative changes in relation to SEND that have brought us to where we are currently today.

Let's look at the Code of Practice in more detail, and how this affects what provision is in place for your child in school currently.

TABLE 1.1 TIMELINE OF SIGNIFICANT POLICY AND LEGISLATION RELATING TO SEND

YEAR	POLICY OR LEGISLATION	OUTLINE/COMMENTS
1981	Education Act 1981	The term 'Special Educational Needs' was introduced, and there was a greater emphasis on integrated provision.
1994		The SENCo role was established in England.
1997	Green paper: Excellence for All	This paper adopted the principle of inclusion as an extension of the capacity of mainstream schools.
2001	Special Educational Needs and Disabilities Act 2001 (SENDA)	This covered disabled people's rights within the provision of education.
2010	The Equality Act 2010	This act consolidated acts in relation to discrimination.
2014	The Children and Families Act 2014	A commitment to improve services for all children regardless of their background. It outlined specific duties on schools to support all children with SEN.
2014	SEND Code of Practice	Outlined the duties for SEND in schools under the new law.
2015	SEND Code of Practice updates	Revisions were made to the Code of Practice, and is the version that is currently in place today.
2022	SEND review green paper	This paper acknowledged that change was needed using the phrase 'right support, right place, right time.'
2023	SEND and Alternative Provision (AP) Improvement Plan	The improvement plan sets out the next steps for SEND provision in schools – the link to this document is in the 'further reading' section of the chapter.

THE CODE OF PRACTICE: THE DEVELOPING LANDSCAPE

The Code of Practice is statutory guidance for educational organisations and establishments such as schools, nurseries and colleges, which means it is what schools and Local Authorities must do to comply with the law. It applies to all maintained schools, academies and free schools. The terminology is a little confusing because it uses the words "statutory" and "guidance" but it means that although it is a guidance document, it contains the legal requirements and guidelines that are set out in the Children and Families Act 2014, the Equality Act 2010, and the Special Educational Needs and Disabilities Regulations 2014. The code includes:

+ Details of the legal requirements that must be followed without exception, and
+ Statutory guidance that must be followed unless there is good reason not to.

It outlines legal obligations so that schools, governors and Local Authorities (LAs) can be held to account if this is not followed, which is really important for your child. The Code of Practice is implemented to ensure that there is a consistent approach across the country, and to reduce the chance of a postcode lottery and difference in care; however, even nearly a decade on, there are differences depending on provision and availability, and the LA approach, as you will know from your own experiences.

So, what are the key points that the Code of Practice sets out directly for schools?

It states that all children and young people are entitled to an appropriate education, and that "every school is required to identify and address the SEN of the pupils that they support" (CoP, 2015) by:

+ Ensuring that children and young people with SEND engage in the activities of the school alongside pupils that do not have SEND.
+ Designating a teacher to be responsible for co-ordinating SEND provision; the SEND Co-ordinator or SENCo.
+ Informing parents when they are making special educational provision for a child.
+ Preparing a SEND information report that contains the arrangements for the admission of disabled children, the steps that are being taken to prevent disabled children from being treated less favourably than others, the facilities provided to enable access to the school for disabled children, and their accessibility plan that illustrates how they plan to improve access progressively over time.
+ Identifying SEND children on a SEND register with provision mapping in place, outlining the provision available for each child.
+ Training staff to help them identify and support children with SEND to ensure early identification of their needs.

SEND pupils are categorised into one 'broad area of need' from of the following;

+ Communication and interaction.
+ Cognition and learning.
+ Social, emotional and mental health difficulties.
+ Sensory and/or physical needs.

Even though your child will be allocated first to one particular area of need, it is recognised that there may be overlapping areas of need, and these will be outlined on any support plan that is in place.

COMPLEX NEEDS

As a parent, you may have a good understanding of your own child's special educational need, disability or complex needs. The following section will give an overview of the different terminology relating to complex needs.

Moderate Learning Difficulties (MLD)

Children with moderate learning difficulties have significant challenges in developing basic literacy and numeracy skills. They may also have other areas of development which are behind their peers, such as having a speech and language delay, a lack of social skills, poor concentration, and low self-esteem. A child's progress will be at least two to three years behind their peers despite a range of appropriate interventions and support being implemented, and they will have a general delay, rather than having specific learning delays as outlined in one of the upcoming sections. Children with MLD generally attend mainstream schools, but some may attend a special school.

Specific Learning Difficulties (SpLD)

A specific learning difficulty is when there is an area of cognition that is affected, and a child finds particularly challenging. Assessments will highlight this difficulty and support can be tailored around this. Most commonly SpLDs in school will be either dyslexia, dyscalculia, or dyspraxia. Children with a SpLD may excel in other areas and subjects, and their progress may be high for some things. SpLD may stand alone or be co-occurring with conditions such as ADHD or autism. Children may also have difficulty with short-term memory and organisation.

Severe Learning Difficulty or Disability (SLD)

Children with SLD have significant cognitive difficulties. They will have difficulty accessing and participating in the school curriculum and will need carefully adjusted support for their needs. They may also have mobility and coordination difficulties, and challenges with communication, independence and social skills. Some children may have difficulty using speech and language, some will be able to hold simple conversations, others may use signs and symbols such as Makaton, or a picture exchange system.

Profound and Multiple Learning Difficulty (PMLD)

Children with PMLD have complex learning needs. They will have severe learning difficulties, combined with physical disabilities, possible medical conditions and sensory challenges. Children with PMLD will need a high level of support from adults for learning needs and for personal everyday care. The curriculum is likely to consist of sensory stimulation and small steps. Verbal communication will be limited and include gestures, pointing, simple language and through support systems.

Complex Learning Difficulties or Disabilities (CLDD)

Children with CLDD have co-existing conditions and difficulties. These conditions overlap and therefore create a complex profile of needs. These children will have challenges in areas of mental health, relationships, behaviour, medical, physical, sensory, communication and cognitive. Progress in the curriculum may be inconsistent for these pupils.

THE SEND AND ALTERNATIVE PROVISION (AP) IMPROVEMENT PLAN

In 2023, a 16-week consultation with schools and parents took place around SEND provision in schools. From this, the SEND and AP Improvement Plan (2023) was developed and published. It outlines the government's proposals of improving SEND pupil outcomes through;

- Improving experiences for families, reducing the current adversity and frustration that they face.
- Deliver financial sustainability of the system.
- Relieve pressure on the current Alternative Provision sector.

They have developed their mission to:

◆ Fulfil children's potential: children and young people with SEND enjoy their child-hood, achieve good outcomes and are well prepared for adulthood and employment.
◆ Build parent's trust: parents and carers experience a fairer, easily navigable sys-tem (across education, health and care) that restores their confidence that their children will get the right support, in the right place, at the right time.
◆ Provide financial sustainability: local leaders make the best use of record invest-ment in the high needs budget to meet children and young people's needs and improve outcomes, while placing local authorities on a stable financial footing.

(DfE, 2023)

At the time of writing, the SEND and AP Improvement Plan is at a very early stage of implementation. There will be many challenges ahead, and discussions with government, schools, SENCos and families on the realities of the implementation will be ongoing. As the next few years develop, and with possible changes in government, it will be important to keep a close eye on the developments and express your own thoughts and give your feed-back to schools and Local Authorities to ensure that the implementation and settling in of the new plans support your own individual child.

Currently, there are no imminent changes to legislation, the assessment needs that are discussed in Chapter 3 will stay the same, and how to apply for an Education, Health and Care plan as outlined in Chapter 5 will stay the same. However, there is clear direction that the DfE will be looking at reducing the number of EHC plans through securing and develop-ing provision within schools that should be "Ordinarily Available" to all pupils and will sup-port many SEND pupils without the need for an EHC plan.

The DfE is developing a set of National Standards for SEND, and they are working with Local Authorities, health professionals, education professionals, practitioners, parents, carers and young people to develop these. They will be tested with regional partners before being imple-mented Nationally. There is a SEND and AP roadmap, which has a projected timeline for the implementation of changes and the link to this is in the further reading section of this chapter.

EXPECTATIONS OF THE LOCAL AUTHORITY (LA)

The Local Authority (LA) has a key role and legal responsibilities in providing support and provision for your child with SEND. They have a legal duty to identify and assess the special educational needs of children that they are responsible for. The LA becomes respon-sible for a child when they become aware that a pupil may have or has SEND.

First, your child's setting such as a nursery, school or college, has a responsibility to support your child with SEND. However, if the setting believes that a pupil needs more sup-port than the setting can give them, then a referral can be made to the LA for an Education, Health and Care Needs Assessment (EHCNA). This assessment could then lead to an

Education, Health and Care Plan (EHCP or EHC plan) which is discussed in detail in Chapter 5. The EHC plan will set out the additional support that your child needs within their school setting. Once this provision has been specified in an EHC plan, it is a legal document, and the LA has a legal duty to ensure that this provision is provided to your child.

The LA must also publish something called the "Local Offer", which is a website which contains a list of all the services and support that they expect children and families with SEND will be able to draw upon for support. It will include all the services that are available within their geographical area of the LA, and also services outside their own LA that children, families and schools are able to access. It might include services such as therapy, care placements or independent schools. This list should not just be a list of links, but will provide details on what settings will provide from the SEND funding, what training provision will include, what transport arrangements will be provided, and what support will be provided for adulthood and independent living. It is important to note that the Local Offer is not legally binding, and there is no guarantee that something listed in the offer will be available.

INCLUSION AND DIFFERENT SETTINGS FOR SEND PUPILS (OUTSIDE A MAINSTREAM SETTING)

All schools have a responsibility to provide appropriate support to children with SEND. Some children will need further specialist support beyond what a mainstream school can provide. Every school must have a designated teacher for co-ordinating the SEND provision, and this is the SENCo. Further guidance on the role and responsibilities of the SENCo are outlined in Chapter Two. The SENCo must inform parents when special educational provision is put in place for a pupil within their school.

Children that are placed in a mainstream school with SEND must be able to access activities and a "broad and balanced curriculum" (CoP, 2015) alongside their peers without SEND, and it is the responsibility of the school to ensure that arrangements are in place for this access. SEND pupils should be able to access a full range of the curriculum subjects and content, and reasonable adjustments made to support pupils to access this. These adjustments will be explored further later in this book. A member of the school's governing body should be assigned to having a specific oversight of the school's provision for SEND pupils, and school leaders and the governing body should review this provision regularly.

The next sections will look at the different alternative types of school provision.

Special Schools

Approximately two percent of pupils attend a special school, with the majority having an EHC plan. Special schools provide education for children with a special educational need or disability. They are a type of school that caters for pupils that cannot access education in a mainstream setting because of their learning difficulty or disability, and whose parents or carers have requested a special school placement and the Local Authority has agreed to arranging this place. Special schools can be a maintained school, an academy or an independent school. The age ranges of pupils vary in special schools, some educate pupils from the age of 3 to 19 (and even up to 25), with others focussing on primary or secondary age phases.

Some special schools will support your child with a broad range of needs, and others will focus around a category as outlined in the CoP and listed in the section on the CoP later in this chapter. Some schools will focus on autism, or speech and language needs, or have a hub or base within a school for these areas. Mainstream schools may also have a base such as this within their school.

Special schools will have a higher staff ratio to pupils than mainstream schools and class sizes are normally smaller, with teachers and teaching assistants likely to have more specialist training in SEND. They will also have access to, and provide a range of services and interventions which will include a speech and language therapist who may be trained in the use of visual communication systems or Makaton, physiotherapist and a school nurse. Many special schools will also have specialist equipment and rooms that mainstream schools do not have, such as a therapy pool, sensory rooms, and adapted outdoor play equipment or gym equipment.

Positives of a special school are:

+ A higher staff to pupil ratio with smaller class sizes.
+ Specialist trained teachers.
+ Pupils mix with peers with similar needs and challenges, which supports positive self-esteem and reduces bullying.
+ Specialist therapists.
+ Specialist resources.

There can also be some drawbacks:

+ The school may offer a limited curriculum and fewer qualifications or GCSEs.
+ Pupils may need to travel a longer distance from home.
+ The lack of opportunity for pupils to socialise with a range of peers of their own age or from their home area if they travel to school.

Most pupils at a special school will be required to have an EHC plan in place. Applying for an EHC plan, what happens next, and what if an EHC plan isn't given is looked at in detail in Chapter 5.

REFLECT

Do you currently have an education setting preference for your child? Is it mainstream, a special school or an alternative provision? What are your reasons for this preference? Have you explored all possibilities, or would you benefit from researching other local settings further?

Alternative Provision

An alternative provision arrangement can be made for a pupil when they would not otherwise receive a suitable education based upon their age, aptitude and any SEN they may have. The education arrangements made must be full-time, unless it is deemed that it is in the best interests of the child that a reduced timetable or level of education should be in place, and should only be seen as a temporary measure. The alternative provision should be made in line with their EHCP.

CASE STUDY

Lina attended a mainstream primary school and was in year three. Lina had been living with her grandparents since the age of 4 due to some neglect and household substance use by her parents. Lina was having difficulty regulating her emotions around potential previous trauma, and this was evident in her increasing challenges with behaviour and being able to regulate within a busy classroom environment. There was ongoing support with a range of therapies, but knowing that this would take time to demonstrate an impact, the school and grandparents decided it would be better for Lina to spend time in a smaller provision in a less busy environment.

The school had an on-site facility named "Grow" for pupils such as Lina that needed additional support, with the intention that this was a short-term provision and that Lina would return to mainstream school again in approximately half a term to a term. The provision supported pupils from a number of schools in the local area. A referral was made into the provision, and a space was secured for Lina. Lina spent a term at the provision before being reintegrated back into the mainstream class within Year 4.

When this education is based anywhere other than a school, it is known as an alternative provision. It could include a Pupil Referral Unit (PRU), alternative provision academy or alternative provision free school. Alternative provision may be suitable for a pupil that has barriers to learning associated with a school setting. The above case study demonstrates on-site provision, but this could be located within a different mainstream school to the one that your child is attending.

Pupil Referral Units (PRUs)

PRUs are for children that face barriers within a mainstream school. The LA funds PRUs and it is their responsibility to provide a full-time education to all children. A PRU is an alternative way from mainstream school of doing this. Pupils that attend PRUs are often referred there, as they need greater care and support than their mainstream school can provide for them.

This will include children who:

- Experience Social, Emotional and Mental Health (SEMH) needs.
- Have behavioural challenges relating to SEMH needs.
- Have emotionally based school avoidance (EBSA) to attend school.
- Are permanently excluded from school or are at risk of permanent exclusion.
- Have specific SEND which can be supported better within a PRU.
- Are a new school starter who had missed out on a school placement.
- Are a pregnant or young mother.

Some pupils will have all of their lessons at the PRU, while others will spend part of the time at the PRU and part of the time at a mainstream school. PRUs are not special schools, and cannot provide the same level of educations for pupils with SEND, so this should not be seen as a long-term educational setting for them.

Elective Home Education (EHE)

Any child including those with SEND can be educated at home if parents choose to do this. A parent would notify the school this is what they are going to do, and the pupil would be removed from the school register.

Children could be electively home educated from the age of 5, and may never attend a school setting, or they may be removed from school and taken off roll to be home educated. Home education can work well when regard for the needs of the child has been considered and it is appropriate and well-delivered. Parents may choose EHE because a child is struggling in a school environment, they may have extreme levels of anxiety, have sensory needs or they may be at risk of exclusion, or it may be a choice of the parents through their own beliefs that they can provide a better educational experience than a school setting.

If a child has been withdrawn from a child for EHE, then the school does not need to provide any support. The LA can provide discretionary support, including support for SEND, and once a child is home educated, the LA will look into the suitability of the education being provided for the child. If the education being provided is not deemed suitable, then a School Attendance Order, or an Education Supervision Order can be applied for by the LA to the court.

It is important to note that parents should not be asked by a school to EHE their child. This is something called 'off-rolling' when a child is purposefully taken off a school register, and when this is in the best interest of a school, and not in the best interest of a child, for example, in order to make a school look more positive with data or exam results.

Education Other Than At School (EOTAS)

This is the education of a child outside a formal setting. It differs from EHE in that your child must have an EHC plan to qualify for this, and the LA will support and provide provision for your child. Whereas if you decide to electively home educate, then they will not. With EOTAS the LA have a duty to arrange and fund the provision outlined in the plan, and they remain legally responsible for this.

CASE STUDY

From a Parent with a Year 6 Pupil, Considering the Next Steps for Their Child

Antonio was attending a mainstream primary school, in Year 6. He had been very well supported by the school, which was a small school. Antonio had got to know the school staff really well, and they knew him and his needs. Antonio had a diagnosis of autism, dyslexia and general anxiety. Over the seven years at primary school, Antonio had received support through nurture groups and interventions, and the school had developed a very good supportive relationship with his mum, Maria. The school had gone above and beyond what was expected, and they had spent time gathering evidence for an EHC plan.

As Antonio entered Year 6, the school had applied for an EHC plan for Antonio ready for the additional support that he would need in secondary school.

Maria, had always worried about how Antonio might cope with secondary school, and now that fear was becoming a reality for her. She was worried with the large sizes of secondary schools, and how he might not cope with the noise, the busy environment and the expectations. She thought that he would be better placed within a special school that could meet his needs.

The school SENCo advised Maria that all schools are different for different children, and it would be good for her to arrange visits to each of the local schools to get a feel and understanding of what could be offered to Antonio, and to begin to picture what it might look like.

Maria arranged visits at three local mainstream schools, and a special school for Moderate Learning Difficulties (MLD). She arranged to speak with the SENCo at each school.

On her visit to school A, she arrived to be shown around by a school tutor and was advised that the SENCo was not available to talk with her that day. She found the corridors busy, and a slight feeling of a chaotic environment. She made another appointment to revisit and meet with the SENCo so that she could ask her questions that she had.

She then visited school B. She was excited to visit school B as it had an Autism hub, and she thought that this would be something that could be beneficial to Antonio. However, when she met with the SENCo, she was not given a tour of any SEND rooms, and she was advised that without an EHC plan Antonio would not access the hub (even though he had a diagnosis of autism), and even with an EHC plan time in the hub would be limited and based around specific interventions. She came away feeling very disappointed.

Maria then visited the special school (school C), she visited a class that just had autistic pupils within it, class sizes were small, no more than twelve pupils in them, and the staff ratio was high. There was a really positive learning environment, and additional provisions such as a sensory room. Maria could see how Antonio could fit in well within an autism class, and potentially build some good friendships, which was a concern for her within a mainstream school setting. There were two drawbacks to the school though: the first was that the school was heavily oversubscribed, so it could be

---

difficult to get Antonio in to the school, and the second was the range of subjects and GCSEs that would be on offer. Maria wondered whether Antonio would benefit from a greater range or at a slightly different level.

Maria then visited school D. Here she was met by the SENCo and given a tour of the school. All the way around, the SENCo discussed strategies of support that could be put into place for Antonio such as leaving classes five minutes early so that he could move between lessons before it got busy, or having support from a member of staff to help him with the transitions between classes. The school also had an inclusion hub, and pupils that needed it could attend. This could be before school, at break times and lunchtimes, and sometimes during lessons if lessons were overwhelming, or if a pupil was struggling with being in class. Pupils did not need an EHC plan to use the hub, it was based on a pupil's needs at the time, and it was a flexible approach.

Maria, for the first time, could see how Antonio might be supported, and might cope with a mainstream secondary school, if the right provision was in place for him. She then arranged another visit, this time with Antonio. After further discussion as a family, they decided that they would apply for school D for Antonio, and then if Antonio did not cope well, they could then consider the special school.

The transition to secondary school became a little stressful as there were delays on the EHC plan application due to a lack of Educational Psychologist in the Local Authority, late reports, and staff absence. Therefore, Antonio was not given a place at school D initially, and had to wait until the EHC plan was in place. This did not happen until two weeks before the end of the summer term. However, the school was very supportive and put in additional transition activities during the last two weeks and in September.

Maria is delighted with how Antonio settled in to secondary school and the progress he has made. He has had times where there have been glitches, but Antonio has been supported well, and there is a very experienced team of support staff.

TOP TIPS FROM MARIA

1. Ensure that you arrange visits at the local schools for your child, consider all of the schools, even if you have children already at a school, think of them as individuals, one school may support your child differently to other schools and children.
2. Speak with a SENCo of the new school, and ask them for real examples of how your child might be supported.
3. If you are applying for an EHC plan, apply early for a transition, do not leave it until Year 6, as things can take longer than expected, even when there are statutory responsibilities in place.
4. Keep an open mind to the different schools, do not listen to what others say, each school is different for each child, make your own visits and make your own mind up as to which school will be best for your child, remember, you know them best.

INTERSECTIONALITY

Intersectionality is the interconnection of social categories such as class, ethnicity, gender identity, gender expression, race and religious beliefs, and how they overlap and are applied to an individual in the form of discrimination or disadvantage. It is a way of describing how multiple forms of inequality combine and compound to form an obstacle.

By understanding intersectionality further, we can gain an understanding of the individual differences we all have, the challenges we face, and the impact of the connection of these categories on us. It is important to understand the impact of intersectionality, and how educational professionals may miss an opportunity to support a pupil because of assumptions towards the challenges within a particular category, and miss other underlying factors in addition to SEND needs. For example, Waitoller and Kozleski (2013) describe how a refugee pupil with behavioural challenges is excluded because the school fails to address their identity and instead only supports one area of need. The school supports and provides services in relation to their disability but fails to support sufficiently with learning language and with the possible trauma that the pupil has experienced.

Chandrika Devarakonda (2022) argues that it is 'necessary for professionals to relate to a child through an intersectional lens, taking into consideration their identities before diagnosing their special educational needs and advising appropriate provision.' By understanding and considering intersectionality for all pupils in school, staff can understand the difference between the complexities that individual pupils may encounter.

REFLECT

Consider whether your own child has intersectionality needs. First, think about what you know about their SEND needs and jot them down. Then think about what else might impact upon them making the progress in school that you think that they have the potential to make. What areas might a school not know about or understand, think about the social categories outlined above, and whether any of these could apply to your child, jot them down.

Professional Discussion

With your child's class teacher or SENCo

At your next review meeting, if you have identified an area above that may impact your own child, discuss this with your child's class teacher or SENCo and explore what this means for your child, and what strategies may be put into place to support them.

CHAPTER SUMMARY

The chapter began by looking at the definition of SEND, and what this means within the educational context. It has given an overview of key policy developments which bring us up to date with the current situation of SEND within government and within schools today to provide context for the bigger picture, and outlines the potential developments of the future. The purpose of key documentation including the Code of Practice (2015) was discussed, explaining what it is, the legal requirements, and a forward look at the SEND and AP improvement plan.

There was also an overview of different settings for SEND pupils outside of mainstream settings and the terminology relating to complex needs. The main case study was from Maria, a parent making decisions about a secondary school for her son, Antonio, and how she came to the decision that she made. There are some tips from her to consider when deciding on the best school for your own child.

Expectations and responsibilities of the Local Authority were outlined, and further details in relation to the LA will be discussed in Chapters 2 and 5.

REFLECT

Think back on this chapter, there is a lot of change happening in SEND provision and policy, how might you keep a watch on this change so you know how it might affect your own child and what is happening in school? Are you a member of any social media groups, for example, that would highlight the changes?

GLOSSARY OF KEY TERMS

- ✦ Alternative Provision (AP) - Education that is based anywhere other than a school.
- ✦ Code of Practice (CoP) - Statutory guidance to support pupils with SEND.
- ✦ Education, Health and Care Plan (EHCP) - A legal document containing the provision that is set out for a pupil with SEND.
- ✦ Intersectionality - The interconnection of social categories, for example, class, ethnicity and gender, and the overlapping system of discrimination or disadvantage.
- ✦ Local Offer - The services and support that a Local Authority lists for potential access by families and schools for pupils with SEND.

FURTHER READING

✦ Department for Education (DfE) (2015). *Special Educational Needs and Disabilities Code of Practice; 0 to 25 Years*. DfE. https://assets.publishing.service.gov.uk/government/uploads/system/uploads/attachment_data/file/398815/SEND_Code_of_Practice_January_2015.pdf

✦ Department for Education (DfE) (2023). SEND and Alternative Provision Improvement Plan. https://www.gov.uk/government/publications/send-and-alternative-provision-improvement-plan

✦ Department for Education (DfE) (2023). SEND and Alternative Provision Improvement Plan Roadmap. https://www.gov.uk/government/publications/send-and-alternative-provision-improvement-plan/send-and-alternative-provision-roadmap

✦ Devarakonda, Chandrika (2022). SEND: Looking Through and Intersectionality Lens. https://www.bera.ac.uk/blog/send-looking-through-an-intersectionality-lens

✦ Independent Provider of Special Education Advice (IPSEA). https://www.ipsea.org.uk/

✦ Local Government Association. https://www.local.gov.uk/parliament/briefings-and-responses/send-and-alternative-provision-improvement-plan-2-march-2023

REFERENCES

Department for Education (DfE) (2015). Special Educational Needs and Disabilities Code of Practice; 0 to 25 Years. DfE.

Devarakonda, C. (2022). SEND: Looking Through and Intersectionality Lens. https://www.bera.ac.uk/blog/send-looking-through-an-intersectionality-lens

UK Government (2010). The Equality Act 2010. https://www.legislation.gov.uk/ukpga/2010/15/contents

Waitoller, F. and Kozleski, E. B. (2013). Understanding and dismantling barriers for partnerships for inclusive education: A cultural historical activity theory perspective. *International Journal of Whole Schooling*, 9, 23-42.

CHAPTER 2

WHAT IS THE CODE OF PRACTICE AND WHAT DOES IT MEAN?

THE ROLES AND RESPONSIBILITIES OF SCHOOL STAFF

CHAPTER AIMS

✦ To get a better understanding of the Code of Practice (CoP) through exploring the roles and responsibilities of school staff.

✦ To understand the role and responsibilities of the SENCo in school.

✦ To understand the role and responsibilities that a class teacher has in relation to SEND and how they are supported in these responsibilities by the SENCo.

✦ To understand the role of the Teaching Assistant (TA) and Learning Support Assistant (LSA) in schools.

✦ To understand the role and responsibilities of parents in relation to schools and SEND.

INTRODUCTION

Chapter 1 introduced you to the Code of Practice (CoP) and how this outlines what should be done for your child within school, and the legal responsibilities of the Local Authority (LA). This chapter will explore areas of the CoP in more detail and will be incorporated throughout when looking at the roles and responsibilities of school staff and parents and carers.

Before we move into the main part of the chapter, I am going to introduce you to our case study.

DOI: 10.4324/9781032689159-3

> **CASE STUDY**
>
> Dario is in Year 6 at primary school, he has a diagnosis of autism, and has further additional needs and challenges.
>
> His mother is Martina and his step-father is Leon.
>
> Throughout the chapter, we will refer to Dario so that you can see how the different roles entwine to support Dario.
>
> Although your own child may not be in primary school, they may be in an Early Years setting such as a nursery, or they may be at a secondary school; the discussions around Dario and the roles and responsibilities of those involved can be applied across each year group and setting.

THE CODE OF PRACTICE

As previously mentioned in Chapter 1, the Code of Practice (CoP) is statutory guidance for educational organisations and establishments. Schools follow the CoP when implementing provision for SEND pupils. By exploring the roles and responsibilities of the SENCo and Class Teacher as they are outlined in the CoP, you will be able to gain an understanding of what each person will be doing for your child. It will also clarify what they shouldn't be doing, for example how a Teaching Assistant (TA) or Learning Support Assistant (LSA) is involved in supporting your child, but is not responsible for their progress.

THE ROLE AND RESPONSIBILITIES OF THE SENCO

Every school, regardless of whether it is within an academy or run by the LA, must have a SENCo which is a requirement by law. The SENCo must be a qualified teacher and hold Qualified Teacher Status (QTS), or demonstrate that they are actively working towards becoming a qualified teacher and be able to demonstrate this and the expectation of them completing. The exception of this is within an independent school or an early years setting.

In addition to being a qualified teacher, the SENCo must also gain another qualification; the National SENCo Award (NASENCo), which is a post-graduate qualification equipping them with the knowledge and skills to carry out the role. The government has also introduced a new qualification for SENCos, which is a National Professional Qualification (NPQ) that is part of a set of qualifications that is taken by senior leaders and Head teachers in schools. Either qualification can be taken to meet the requirements set out in the CoP.

Depending on the size of the school, your child's school may have a full-time SENCo, with a SEND team of specialist staff, maybe including a Deputy SENCo, or phase leader SENCos such as an Early Years SENCo, Primary SENCo, or Key Stage 3 and Key Stage 4 SENCo. Other smaller schools may have a SENCo that works part-time, or who is a class teacher for part of the week too, or the Headteacher themselves may take on the role of SENCo as part of their duties and responsibilities. There is no right or wrong way for this to be organised; it will depend on the size of the school and the number of SEND pupils that the school has. It is up to the school how they organise their SEND staffing arrangements, including the SENCo.

The Role of the SENCo

The importance of the role of the SENCo has grown over the last decade. There is value placed on the work that SENCo does to support SEND pupils. As part of their role, the SENCo works closely with the Headteacher to direct the school's SEND policy and improvement plan, and to consider the budgeting aspects of what money is coming in and how it is being spent.

The SENCo also has to report to the school's governing body, who meet termly and oversee the running and governance of the school. The SENCo will produce a report which will include elements such as how the school thinks it is performing in relation to SEND and the Ofsted descriptors*, the number of pupils on the SEN register, and the number that have Education, Health and Care plans (EHC plans), any changes to the SEND policy, the budget for SEND and how it was spent, the staffing for SEND pupils, and if anything has changed, any interventions that have been implemented, and feedback on whether they have worked, Continuous Professional Development (CPD) and training that staff have taken in relation to SEND and how that has supported SEND pupils, whether pupils have had a voice in their support, and if parents and carers have had a voice and been able to share their feedback. It includes details on outside agencies that have been working in the school with pupils, any areas that need further development for SEND and whether there have been any complaints regarding the support of SEND pupils.

> ***What is Ofsted?** Ofsted is a government organisation that stands for the Office for Standards in Education, Children's Services and Skills. They report directly to parliament but they are independent of the Government, and, by law, they must inspect schools with the aim of providing information for parents and carers, as well as promoting improvement and holding schools to account.

The governing body will have a member of their board that is called a SEND governor, and who will have a deeper knowledge of SEND. They will visit the school and meet with the SENCo and their team if they have one, to look at what is going well, and what the challenges are. They will ask questions and listen to how the governing body can support areas of work, for example, this could be agreeing for money to be spent in a particular way on resources, or an additional room being created to support SEND pupils.

The Responsibilities of the SENCo

It is the responsibility of the SENCo to oversee all the daily running of any SEND provision in school on a day to day basis. Although it is their responsibility to oversee it, it is not their responsibility to implement it all, or to undertake every task, conversation or interaction regarding SEND. It is important that everyone working with your child takes responsibility for the implementation and assessment and feedback of various elements of support both within and outside of the classroom.

The sort of activities that the SENCo will carry out will include:

✦ Supporting the identification of SEND pupils through supporting a class teacher or other adults to carry out assessments both within and outside the classroom.
✦ To track and monitor the progress of SEND pupils throughout the school, and follow up and report back on this to staff, services and governors.
✦ To fully co-ordinate the provision of pupils with SEND, overseeing and putting into place the activities that might take place for your child.
✦ They will liaise with parents and carers of pupils with SEND, but this might not be all the time; it could be that your main point of contact is your child's class teacher.
✦ They will liaise with outside agencies and professionals such as the SEND team within the Local Authority, or with professionals who work within a multi-agency team such as family support workers or Educational Psychologists (EPs).
✦ They will ensure that all documents and records relating to the pupils with SEND in their school are accurate and kept up to date.
✦ The SENCo will also lead on the development, the writing of, and then the implementation of the SEND development plan. This will include the next steps for the school in improving their SEND provision, and it will link in with whole school priorities, plans and policies.
✦ The SENCo will write the school's SEND policy which will be reviewed and signed off by the Governing Body, and this should be uploaded to the school website for you to view as a parent.

ACTIVITY

Have a look on your child's school website.

✦ Can you find the SEND policy? Have a read through of this, what does it tell you about the support that your child is receiving?
✦ Are you having meetings when you should be, in line with their policy?
✦ Can you also find the latest SEND report? What does this tell you about how the school is supporting their SEND pupils.

You may find that the SEND policy is incorporated with an inclusion policy, or it may have a slightly different name.

If you have any queries regarding the support that you are getting for your child from their school, it is always a good idea to look at these two documents and see what the process is and whether your child is getting the support that you think they should. Do your ideas align with that which is outlined in the school's policy? If you are unsure, arrange a meeting to talk with someone about it to understand how this relates to your child. Sometimes, it can be a misunderstanding or miscommunication regarding the provision that is available.

The SENCo will have many strategic roles and tasks to do as part of their daily job in a school. This will include:

* Being part of the leadership team, and attending leadership meetings about the whole school.
* They will inform the leadership team and the Governing Body on any policy and practice that is changing or guidance that is given from the government.
* The SENCO will develop the vision and values that the school has for the provision of their SEND pupils.
* They will ensure that their SEND report meets the legal requirements and that this is also published on the school website for you to read as a parent.
* They will undertake training so that they are knowledgeable on the current policy and practice relating to SEND.
* They will take a lead on (in discussion with other leadership staff) making decisions about the deployment of staff to support SEND pupils and the use of resources such as nurture rooms.
* The SENCo will be challenged by the Governing Body on this use of staff and resources to ensure that it is effective and that it is being reviewed.
* The SENCo is responsible for organising and/or delivering training to staff (teachers, Teaching Assistants (TAs) and Learning Support Assistants (LSAs)) and ensuring that all staff know what their role is in relation to supporting their SEND pupils.
* They will observe and ensure that High Quality Teaching (or Quality First Teaching[1] (QTF)) is taking place in classrooms for pupils with SEND.
* They will also liaise with curriculum co-ordinators (such as the lead person for English, maths, history, geography, etc.) to ensure that SEND pupils are able to access every area of the curriculum, and that adjustments are made and there are resources available for each subject so that this can happen.

As you can see from the list above, the SENCo role is a large role, covering strategic elements, and implementation of the daily provision. Taking this into account, you may understand why it can sometimes be a little bit difficult or challenging to arrange a meeting with the SENCo, particularly when they have many SEND pupils within their school.

To ensure that the SENCo has time for all the elements within their role, the Leadership team at the school need to provide time for a SENCo to:

- ❖ Plan and co-ordinate provision, including the deployment of staff.
- ❖ Maintain and update records and paperwork.
- ❖ Teach pupils with SEND.
- ❖ Train staff and TAs and LSAs on interventions and strategies to support pupils.
- ❖ Observe SEND pupils in class.
- ❖ Liaise with settings either side of the school age range ready for transition, including nurseries, secondary schools, colleges and other sixth form provisions.

CASE STUDY

By a Primary School SENCo

My role as a SENCo is varied and challenging, each day is different, and I do my best to support every pupil with SEND in our school. There is normally something I need to find out, a problem to solve, and a celebration to have regarding progress that one of our pupils has made.

I have been a SENCo for many years, and my role has changed over these years. In the past it was my responsibility to carry out all of the reviews and writing targets, and this was unmanageable in a school with many SEND pupils and all of the other things I needed to do. Now, the responsibilities and some of the daily tasks are shared out, and as a school we really understand that it is everyone's role and responsibility to support our SEND pupils and their families.

My day starts with checking up on staffing and support, whether anyone is off ill, and whether the provision is in the right place for the pupils that need it. Sometimes I need to change things and communicate this with staff. Staff and pupils arrive at school, and I check in with key pupils to make sure they have had a smooth transition in to school, Dario is one of these pupils. Sometimes he can find mornings challenging, he doesn't like the busyness of the drop off, so he arrives into school 15 minutes earlier and settles in to the class with a task that has been given to him by the class teacher. This is a provision that is highlighted on his Individual education Plan (IEP). Once the pupils are in and settled, I return to my office to begin with the paperwork and task that I need to do for the day.

First on the list is to organise a review for Dario. We are gathering the paperwork to apply for an Education, Health and Care Needs Assessment (EHCNA) with the Local Authority to see if Dario meets the threshold for an Education, Health and Care plan (EHCP/EHC plan). We think this is important for his next step in transitioning to secondary school. We applied several years ago when Dario was in Key Stage 1, in Year 2, but it was turned down. Over the years we have supported Dario through the provision that we have in school, and we know Dario and his family very well, but we all feel that he may have some difficulty in a larger school, so it is important that we apply for this assessment.

I contact the parents, Dario's mum, step-dad and dad, to see if they can attend. I also contact the family support worker who has been supporting Martina and Leon with some behavioural challenges that are having at home with Dario. A date is arranged for the meeting, this is important as it will gain their latest views on how things are going before we submit the paperwork for the EHCNA.

I then follow up on some referrals that we have made, confirming the arrangements for mental health support for one of our pupils, and another with the speech and language therapist.

As it is Thursday, it is training day for our TAs and LSAs. This is something we have recently implemented, and while there is a whole school singing and choir assembly, the TAs and LSAs have a short training session with me on an area of focus that we have identified through our training and reflection sessions. Today we are looking at supporting SEND pupils with transitioning from the playground back to the classroom, as sometimes it can take our SEND pupils a little longer to settle for many reasons.

Over lunchtime, I check in with staff that have been delivering their morning interventions, and then head to the classrooms to observe pupils and support staff in the afternoon.

The day finishes with an afterschool meeting with a parent, and a senior leader meeting.

My job as a SENCo can be very challenging, and I wish that there were more hours in the day, but supporting SEND pupils and their families gives me a sense of pride and fulfilment. There is still much to learn, and I don't always get things right when I am juggling things.

The role for a secondary SENCo or an Early Years SENCo will be similar in the sort of daily tasks that they cover, it will just be relevant for their age range and setting. In some schools, a SENCo will also be teaching, and it may be a particular subject in secondary schools, and lessons may be incorporated within their day, whereas in a primary school, the SENCo may have set SENCo days and different teaching days.

THE ROLE AND RESPONSIBILITIES OF THE CLASS TEACHER

The role and responsibility of the class teacher may have changed since you were at school yourself. With the implementation of the new SEND Code of Practice (CoP) in 2014, there was a shift in how the SENCo and class role supported pupils with SEND. At the core of the CoP is the understanding that it is everyone's responsibility to support pupils with SEND in school, and this isn't just a job for the SENCo and the TA. This was a huge shift in thinking and how practice looked in schools. Teachers began taking a lead on the support and provision in their class with guidance from the SENCo, and leading on meetings and writing plans and targets for their pupils.

It is the class teacher who is responsible for all of their pupils in their class to make progress. This includes your primary class teacher, and every secondary teacher that your child is with for each subject. If a pupil is taken out of class for an intervention, or some group learning of some sort, then the class teacher should know what this is, what knowledge and skills are being worked on, and how much progress their pupil is making. They should then draw upon this and support practice of these skills back within the classroom. It should never be a TA or LSA that keeps this information to themselves; the teacher should be seeking this information to inform progress and next steps for their pupil.

It is also important that your child is not working with the TA or LSA all of the time, your child's class teacher should be working with them regularly too. They should be assessing your child's progress, and also teaching them, giving them input, as they are the qualified teacher, and your child has a right to receive teaching from their qualified teacher. Pupils can also become attached to a particular one-to-one support person, and this in itself can cause some difficulties which are discussed further in Chapter 3.

Responsibilities of the Class Teacher

The Code of Practice outlines a very long list of the responsibilities of the class teacher, which include:

- ❖ Teachers are responsible and accountable for the progress and development of all the pupils in their class; this includes where pupils access support from TAs, LSAs and specialist staff.
- ❖ The class teacher(s) should work with all of the children on a daily basis, with SEND pupils, this is even when an intervention group, or one-to-one teaching is happening away from the classroom or main subject teacher.
- ❖ The class teacher(s) should work closely with TAs and LSAs or specialist staff to plan and assess the impact of an intervention or support group and how this teaching or intervention links back to the teaching that is happening within the classroom.
- ❖ The class teacher(s) should work with the SENCo to revise the support for the pupil once they have assessed the pupil's progress. They would then decide on any changes or adjustments that need to be made to the support that is in place, and the outcomes made. These changes should be in consultation and discussion with the parents or carers and pupil.

The class teacher responsibilities that are in relation to pupils with SEND fall into three categories:

1. Working directly with pupils at risk of, or with Special Educational Needs/Disabilities through identification, assessment, intervention, monitoring and review.
2. Working with families of pupils with SEND.
3. Working with other professionals to support pupils with SEND.

These three areas are outlined in further detail below.

For pupils that are at risk of, or have, Special Educational Needs or Disabilities, class teachers also have a long list of things that they should be doing. These include:

- Identifying special educational needs and barriers to pupils' learning.
- Selecting appropriate interventions (in discussion with the SENCo).
- Follow appropriate processes and actions when identifying a pupil with SEND, such as following the graduated approach (this is discussed in detail in Chapter 3).
- Have full knowledge and understanding of pupils' Individual Education Plans (IEPs).
- Have full knowledge and understanding of pupils' Education and Health Care plans (EHC plans).
- Provide access for pupils to a broad and balanced curriculum.
- Understand what High Quality Teaching is and provide this to pupils.
- Have high expectations for pupils based on their assessments.
- Be responsible and accountable for pupil learning, progress and development.
- Work with pupils on a daily basis.
- Regularly assess, monitor and review pupil progress, including social, emotional and mental needs of pupils.
- Take up their own professional development to secure their knowledge, understanding and skills in relation to SEND.

The Graduated Approach is an assessment cycle for pupils that have or may have SEND. This is discussed in detail in the next chapter, Chapter 3. As part of this approach, class teachers will also hold the responsibility of:

- Informing and involving parents and carers at the point that they and the SENCo have initial concerns regarding a child's learning, progress, and possible special educational needs.
- Class teachers should develop a dialogue with parents and carers to support progress and outcomes.
- When a pupil is receiving SEND support, the class teacher should talk to parents regularly (more than just at review meetings) to update parents on an informal basis and also produce an annual report on pupil progress.
- Adjustments, interventions and support should be put into place and monitored and reviewed by the class teacher.
- The class teacher may seek the involvement of specialists.
- EHC plans should be reviewed at least once per year, with targets updated.
- There should be a clear date for review, and parents and carers should be notified of this well in advance so that they can attend. Parents and carers should be given clear information about the impact of the support and interventions that are in place, or have been provided, and they should be involved in planning the next steps for their child.

Working with families, class teachers (or the SENCo) must:

- Formally notify parents where it is decided to provide a pupil with SEND support, although the parents or carers and the pupil should have already been involved in forming the initial assessment of needs.
- Contribute at least annually to a review of an EHC plan when one is in place.
- Produce an annual report for parents and carers annually.

When working with other professionals, class teachers should:

- Receive advice and support from the SENCo in assessing the pupil, problem-solving, and implementing support for the pupil.
- Receive guidance from the SENCo in revising or adjusting the support that is in place depending upon the outcomes and effectiveness of that support on progress and development of the pupil.
- Work closely with support staff such as TAs and LSAs to plan and assess the impact of any interventions or support that has been put into place for a pupil.
- Work with other professionals collaboratively who work outside of the school, for example, from health, social care, medical or mental health, to improve special educational needs identification and support for pupils through implementing advised strategies, approaches and resources.

CASE STUDY

A Class Teacher's Role in Working with Dario

I am Dario's class teacher, he has recently started in Year 6 and we are half a term in to the year. We are having regular reviews with the SENCo (more than we would normally have) as we are ensuring that as much paperwork is in place for us to apply for an Education and Health Care Needs Assessment (EHCNA).

Dario has a diagnosis of autism, and he has challenges with new routines and environments, and when things are changed without prior warning. This can lead to him becoming upset quickly and sometimes angry, but he doesn't mean to be angry, it is his way of saying he is scared and he doesn't like the change.

I know Dario well, as I was also his class teacher in Year 3. I remember that he had been getting general support through High Quality Teaching in Key Stage 1 in the adjoining infant school that he was attending. But when he joined the junior school, he struggled with the change of environment and the new routines. This is when I worked with the SENCo and Dario's mum and step-dad to start identifying and assessing his needs. I had regular discussions with the SENCo about what strategies and support we were putting in place for Dario, for example, he was attending a lunchtime club to support the development of social skills, we were then implementing what Dario was learning in this, within the classroom, supporting him to recall strategies that he could try. Dario was also having daily time tables rehearsal to develop his confidence and recall skills.

We met with his parents to discuss what we were doing, and what was working, and what wasn't. It was also good to speak with his family to find out what worked and didn't work at home so that we could join up with our thinking and strategies to make it easier for Dario as he likes consistency.

We started on the graduated approach (discussed in Chapter 3) and began to implement a further level of support for Dario than we had solely in class. Dario was supported through interventions including the use of an online intervention programme supporting the mastery of essential reading skills. This intervention happened three times a week for 20 minutes. Other pupils in the class were also doing this, and they liked the computer programme and saw it as being a fun activity to take part in.

As a class teacher I was very much in charge of what Dario was doing (with the support of the SENCo), and I knew what he was working on. I would then use this within my own planning and ensure that he was implementing his new skills in our other lessons.

Dario has continued to progress with support through the graduated approach, and the interventions in place, and he was referred to a paediatrician. Dario received a diagnosis of autism a year ago.

Now we are in Year 6, and although Dario is making progress, he is not making progress that is as quick as his peers, and he struggles with anxiety and his mental health. He has twice had support from Child and Adolescent Mental Health Services (CAMHS).

Current targets for Dario are:

❖ Working to reduce Dario's load to cope with more difficult tasks
❖ Continue developing skills to support solving maths problems
❖ Support Dario to articulate his feelings and recognise his triggers in difficult situations

These are then broken down into SMART targets (Specific, Measurable, Achievable, Relevant and Time-bound) so that we know what we are working on, and how we will know what progress is being made.

For example:

❖ *Working to reduce Dario's load to cope with more difficult tasks*

> **S** - When giving Dario a difficult maths task, the LSA will ensure that Dario is working in a quiet environment with no distractions
> **M** - This will happen at each maths lesson for the next half term, we will measure how Dario copes with the tasks
> **A** - The LSA will take Darion to the small room next to the main classroom to work on the individual activity part of the lesson
> **R** - We will be seeing if by reducing the sensory impact of the busy classroom will have an impact on Dario coping with the maths tasks
> **T** - We will review this after half a term to look at the impact

I am reviewing the targets for Dario at this meeting, and I am working with the SENCo to gather paperwork such as Dario's views on how he is getting on at school, and observations from myself as the teacher in the form of a checklist of his strengths and difficulties, emotional literacy and behaviour.

This paperwork is then going to be sent off with Dario's EHCNA application.

We will continue to work on Dario's targets and reviewing them, and we have started to think about what transition will need to look like to support Dario moving up to secondary school. Early links with the school for school visits will be needed, and supporting Dario to know the school layout, and his key support staff.

THE ROLE AND RESPONSIBILITIES OF THE TEACHING ASSISTANT (TA) AND LEARNING SUPPORT ASSISTANT (LSA)

What Is the Difference between a Teaching Assistant (TA) and Learning Support Assistant (LSA)?

There are many similarities between the two roles, and often the terms of the two roles will be used interchangeably.

◆ A TA will tend to work across the whole class offering academic support to all pupils and being a good role model to them.
◆ An LSA will often work one-to-one with pupils, they may have a pastoral role, and support the implementation and conducting interventions.

However, as I have said, often the roles are interchangeable, and you may have staff working in your child's class that work across the class or with particular pupils. In secondary school, TAs/LSAs may work within a subject department, and your child may see several different support staff over the course of the day.

There is a document that has been produced called "The professional Standards for Teaching Assistants". This is a document written by an independent panel that was formulated by the Department for Education (DfE) in 2016. It consisted of Union representatives and educational experts, and the panel was tasked with clarifying roles and responsibilities of TAs and the workforce.

The Standards are not compulsory in school, but they are strongly recommended by the teaching unions to be implemented and adhered to within schools. Although the Standards were developed in the UK, they highlight the core values and skills for the Teaching Assistant and Learning Support Assistant roles.

A great deal of your work that a TA or LSA does is working with SEND pupils on a one-to-one basis, working with small groups within classes or implementing specialist-focused interventions.

Working with Pupils on a One-to-One Basis

A TA or LSA may have all of their time allocated to working with one specific pupil on a one-to-one basis. Or they may work with a pupil within a group or a whole class setting, or they may need to give a pupil additional support at particular periods throughout the day.

The Education Endowment Foundation (EEF, 2018) researches key areas in schools, and it produced a document looking at how TAs were used in schools and gave recommendations on how they can work effectively. This document highlights that working directly with a pupil on a one-to-one basis 100% of the time is not good practice. It can lead to challenges such as the pupil becoming reliant upon one person, having expectations of support at all times, and it can prevent them from building up independent working and resilience. Some parents or carers may have an expectation that their child should have a one-to-one person working with them at all times, but this is not effective and can be detrimental to a child making progress and developing independent working skills.

At times though, it is necessary, and vital for progress. One-to-one support might be:

◆ The TA/LSA checking in on your child to set out the expectations and timetable for the day, ensuring that your child understands what is to follow throughout the day and what lessons will be taking place.
◆ The TA/LSA may need to support facilitation of the unstructured times of the day such as the transition times between lessons, and break times and lunch times.
◆ The TA/LSA may need to give hover support when a pupil is working on a task in class, checking in with them, looking over what they are doing, where they are at, and offering encouragement and praise to keep them on track or motivated. Your child will be working towards independence, so the balance of this may change from lesson to lesson and over time.
◆ Hover support may include some taught elements when needed.
◆ The TA/LSA will need to know the pupil's IEP or EHCP targets, and how what they are doing is supporting your child working towards these.
◆ The TA/LSA will need to feedback regularly to your child's class teacher. Your child is the class teacher's responsibility, and communication between the teacher and TA/LSA is key so that informed decisions can be made around reviewing their progress, and adjusting the provision that they are receiving.

The TA/LSA may work with SEND pupils through implementing specific intervention programmes.

There are many types of intervention programmes that may be happening in your child's school. Here is an overview of some of the interventions that may be taking place.

INTERVENTION PROGRAMMES

Behaviour Interventions

Behaviour interventions are normally carried out when a pupil is having difficulty regulating emotions and presenting with behaviour that challenges. They may have an EHCP and a target about managing their behaviour too. A member of support staff could carry out intervention work relating to specific strategies for a pupil to recognise when they are beginning to dysregulate, and when emotions are becoming unmanageable and therefore affecting the outward behaviour then seen in the classroom. The TA/LSA should be trained in working with the pupil on strategies, and a support plan be put into place that gives clear guidance on the process and strategies to be used.

Collaborative Interventions

Group interventions will enable groups of pupils to rehearse subject content and knowledge through group discussions and teamwork. Pupils will be given the opportunity to listen to the contributions of other pupils which can help them generate or confirm their own ideas, or challenge their thoughts and develop new thinking around a topic or area of discussion. Group interventions will deliver a specific programme based on gaps in curriculum knowledge and skills.

One-to-One Intervention

This targeted support identifies specific areas of content knowledge and skills in which a pupil has gaps in. These interventions provide the opportunity for a pupil to work directly and individually with a TA or LSA on very personalised targets, and there is greater scope and achievement of accelerated learning via one-to-one interventions. These types of interventions are normally implemented in short bursts of approximately 20 minutes a session with several sessions a week.

Classroom Based Interventions

Classroom based interventions can be an effective strategy to support the development of pupils in a structured way without being removed from the class base. This can have positive effects on pupils as they are not seen as being singled out for additional support in the same way when they are removed from the class. It also minimises disruption for the pupils as part of their day. As you will see, this has benefits for SEND pupils as they will be staying in the same environment, with less change. However, distraction from other pupils and other teaching that may be happening at the same time will need to be considered.

Social, Emotional and Well-Being Interventions

Some interventions will not be based on academic progress and will be centred around pupils' social, emotional health and well-being, which is just as important. Some pupils may have experienced trauma or loss, and intervention groups within schools for a group of pupils may be held. It is a safe space for pupils to explore their thoughts, feelings and share experiences with pupils and adults. These groups may include a grief or loss group, a nurture group, an exam anxiety group or communication skills group. These are just a few examples.

Peer Tutoring

Peer tutoring is more common in secondary school settings. This is when a more experienced peer buddies up with a less experienced peer to provide some tutoring and support in a specific area of development. Both the peer tutor and the tutee will benefit from this, developing their own personal skills. A peer tutoring programme will need to be facilitated and overseen by a support member of staff, with progress being monitored and the match between the peer tutor and tutee observed to ensure that any difficulties are worked through. There are many benefits of peer tutoring for SEND pupils. Often, SEND pupils prefer to work with an adult rather than their peers, as they feel safer with direction from an adult. Peer tutoring can bridge this gap with a mentor that is experienced, and often a little older than themselves.

Metacognition and Self-Regulation Interventions

Intervention programmes that focus on metacognition and self-regulation concentrate on pupils thinking about their learning. This type of programme might concentrate on specific areas such as self-management, evaluation of work, setting goals for themselves, monitoring their progress, and motivating their learning.

CASE STUDY

An LSA Working with Dario

I work with Dario on a daily basis, but I also work with the rest of the class and support the class teacher in many ways. During the input of a lesson, I often sit with two or three different pupils and check on their understanding of what is being taught, and help them to discuss their ideas which they can find tricky, particularly Dario as he doesn't like discussing his ideas with the other pupils. I can step in and facilitate the discussion, or Dario can share his ideas with me.

When we move to table work, I often work with Dario to check in with him, but I don't sit with him all the time. I move around the group and do "hover support" which is where I keep an eye on him, and a couple of other pupils, checking that they are able to start the task, and understand what is being asked of them. Sometimes I will sit with Dario to go into something in more detail. The class teacher will also be doing this, and sometimes she will sit with Dario or their group, and I will sit with another group and be working on something with them.

At the moment, I am delivering a six-week maths intervention programme. Dario is part of a small group that I take out of class for 15 minutes, three times a week. We do this straight after lunch while the class is getting ready for the afternoon lessons and doing register; this way it doesn't take out any time from his other curriculum subjects.

In a secondary school setting, an LSA or TA will work in a similar way within a classroom, but they may be allocated to a department or subject, so your child may see different support staff in different classrooms rather than one LSA be following a class. In the way that secondary class teachers are subject specialists, the LSA or TA will be knowledgeable about the subject that they are working with. In some cases, LSAs or TAs will be allocated to individual pupils, or they will work in a hub environment and go out to support pupils as needs change on a daily basis.

THE ROLE AND RESPONSIBILITIES OF THE PARENT OR CARER

As a parent, it can be difficult and challenging time supporting their child with SEND. It can be stressful when communicating feelings with the school, or understanding what support is in place when you can see that your child is having difficulties.

I have gathered the views of some parents and carers to draw up the top tips below:

TOP TIPS

- Attend meetings that are scheduled, in person if possible, as this will give you the opportunity to ask questions or hear discussions with staff.
- Take the time to read any paperwork before meetings, and highlight areas that you don't understand.
- If you are not confident in asking questions in a meeting, write them down and give them to the class teacher or SENCo before the meeting so that they can be included and answered.
- Work with the school to find solutions for any challenges with your child, and share ideas that you have from home.
- Gain an understanding of what the school can and cannot do. The school has its own challenges with staffing and funding, and often it is doing their best to find solutions around this.
- Have regular contact with your child's class teacher, find out what has gone well during the week, don't just focus on what hasn't gone well.
- Celebrate the things going well, even if they are small steps.

Chapter 7 will be looking at how to get the most from meetings in schools.

CHAPTER SUMMARY

This chapter has outlined the long list of roles and responsibilities of the SENCo, Class teacher, and the Teaching Assistant (TA) and Learning Support Assistant (LSA). It shows how the roles link, cross over and who is responsible for the learning and development of your child. There are some top tips for you to consider when working with the school, and areas of these will be expanded upon in Chapter 7.

REFLECT

Think back on this chapter. How is your child supported in school?

- Who do you have regular meetings with, is it the class teacher or the SENCo?
- Does the TA/LSA support your child in school, is this in the classroom or through interventions?
- Is there anything you are not sure about that you would like to ask your class teacher or SENCo?

GLOSSARY OF KEY TERMS

- Ofsted – The Office for Standards in Education, Children's Services and Skills. Ofsted is a government organisation. They report directly to parliament but they are independent of the Government, and, by law, they must inspect schools with the aim of providing information for parents and carers, as well as promoting improvement and holding schools to account.
- Special Educational Needs Coordinator (SENCo) – Works within a school to co-ordinate the provision for pupils with SEND.
- Teaching Assistant – A TA will tend to work across the whole class offering academic support to all pupils and being a good role model to them.
- Learning Support Assistant – An LSA will often work one-to-one with pupils, they may have a pastoral role, and support the implementation and conducting interventions.

FURTHER READING AND REFERENCES

- Department for Education (2016). *The Professional Standards for Teaching Assistants*. Department for Education (DfE).

❖ Education Endowment Foundation (2018). Making Best Use of Teaching Assistants. https://educationendowmentfoundation.org.uk/education-evidence/guidance -reports/teaching-assistants?utm_source=/education-evidence/guidance-reports /teaching-assistants&utm_medium=search&utm_campaign=site_searchh &search_term

❖ Education Endowment Foundation (2021). One to One Tuition. https://educationen dowmentfoundation.org.uk/education-evidence/teaching-learning-toolkit/one-to -one-tuition

❖ Webster, R. (2022). *The Inclusion Illusion*. UCL Press.

NOTE

1 The term High Quality Teaching is replacing Quality First Teaching in schools, but many schools refer to both or to QFT still at the time of writing.

PART II

SUPPORT FOR YOUR CHILD IN SCHOOL

CHAPTER 3

HOW YOUR CHILD IS ASSESSED IN SCHOOL

THE GRADUATED APPROACH

CHAPTER AIMS

❖ To understand the types of assessment in schools and their purpose.
❖ To gain an understanding of current SEND practice in schools that is taking place for your child, including High Quality Teaching for all, Ordinarily Available provision for all, and targeted support.
❖ To gain an understanding of what adaptive teaching in the classroom is.
❖ To gain an understanding of the graduated approach, and the teacher and parents/carers role is in this process.
❖ To understand the importance of your child's voice and how this is incorporated within the graduated approach cycle.

Professional Discussion

Before we move on to look at how your child is assessed, did you have any questions from the reflection at the beginning of the chapter? If so, note these down and arrange a time to speak with your child's class teacher about them. It will help you and your child if you have a good understanding of how your school staffing works to support your child.

❖ You might like to think about how your child is supported in class, what is the role of the TA/LSA for your child?
❖ What are the next steps for your child, what targets are they working on?
❖ Or, who is the best person to contact if you have any concerns or worries?

INTRODUCTION

There are many forms of assessments and tests in school, it is important to have an understanding of what your child might be doing, to help you to understand what stress they may be under, or to know what assessments they may be doing to help them to get the right support. It will also help you to understand what the class teacher or SENCo is referring to in meetings, and why and how something is implemented to support your child.

THE TYPES AND PURPOSE OF ASSESSMENT IN SCHOOL

There are two main types of assessment that happen in school on a daily basis, they are formative assessment and summative assessment. These will be explained in further detail now.

Formative Assessment

Formative assessment happens on a daily basis and it forms part of reviewing what is planned and taught to your child. Formative assessment includes the teacher asking open and closed questions, quizzes, polls, self-assessment (your child checking their own work) and peer-assessment (checking the work of a friend). This type of assessment is part of live monitoring, and feeds in to the teachers planning for the following day so that they can support pupil progress on a daily and lesson by lesson basis.

Summative Assessment

Summative assessment happens at the end of a period or block of teaching, such as at the end of a half term or term, or the end of a particular topic or unit of work. Formal summative assessment results in examinations such as Standardised Assessment Tests (SATs) that your child will experience in primary schools, or General Certificate of Secondary Education (GCSEs) at the end of pupils' secondary education. A table of summative assessment points is presented later in the chapter.

SEND PRACTICE AND SUPPORT IN SCHOOLS

High Quality Teaching

High Quality Teaching (HQT) is a term used for the good quality of teaching that should be happening in a classroom on a daily basis. This teaching should have high expectations for all pupils and be available to all pupils. This is also really important for your child with SEND. Teaching and assessment are intrinsically linked, the assessment of pupils is running through everything that your child is taught, and at each stage of planning, delivery, and review of each lesson that your child's class teacher delivers.

This is why it is important to look at these elements now, before we move on to the graduated approach.

The DfE Code of Practice (2015) states:

> High quality teaching that is differentiated and personalised will meet the individual needs of the majority of children and young people. Some children and young people need educational provision that is additional to or different from this. This is special educational provision under Section 21 of the Children and Families Act 2014. Schools and colleges must use their best endeavours to ensure that such provision is made for those who need it. Special educational provision is underpinned by high quality teaching and is compromised by anything less.

Adaptive Teaching

Adaptive teaching forms part of High Quality Teaching. Adaptive teaching sets the same targets, goals and objectives for all pupils, aiming for the top, and then provides different levels of scaffolded support to pupils who need this. This should be part of High Quality Teaching and what is ordinarily available to all pupils. The scaffolding then targets pupil starting points to support their progress. These scaffolds are taken away as the pupil becomes more proficient in the concept, process or knowledge being taught.

High Quality Teaching forms the base layer of the model shown in Figure 3.1. This is the support for all pupils, all of the time.

A Model of High Quality Teaching

Targeted Academic Support

Forming the next layer of the model is Targeted Academic Support, which is a level above provision such as HQT for all pupils. Most pupils will benefit from the focus on high quality, whole-class teaching. However, some children may require extra, targeted support that is tailored to their specific needs and to support then to get their learning back on track when they have a gap in their knowledge or have fallen behind in a particular area.

Additional interventions could include revisiting foundational knowledge, practising core skills or pre-learning upcoming content for lessons. Interventions need to complement and link to the curriculum being covered within the class.

Wider Strategies

Wider strategies form the top layer of the pyramid in Figure 3.1. This layer includes strategies to improve positive learning behaviours and support to move pupils back on track when there is a non-academic barrier such as poor attendance, or highly personalised interventions that may be from a specialist professional.

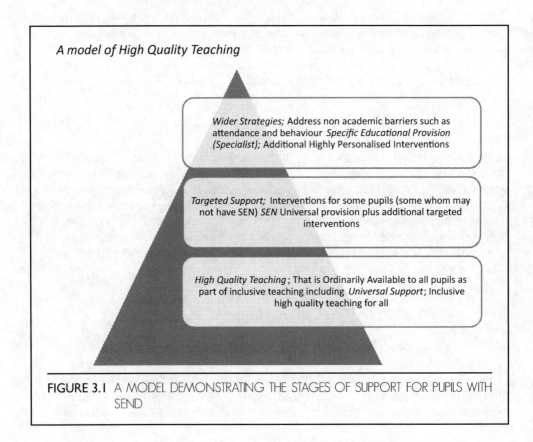

A model of High Quality Teaching

Wider Strategies; Address non academic barriers such as attendance and behaviour *Specific Educational Provision (Specialist);* Additional Highly Personalised Interventions

Targeted Support; Interventions for some pupils (some whom may not have SEN) *SEN* Universal provision plus additional targeted interventions

High Quality Teaching ; That is Ordinarily Available to all pupils as part of inclusive teaching including *Universal Support;* Inclusive high quality teaching for all

FIGURE 3.1 A MODEL DEMONSTRATING THE STAGES OF SUPPORT FOR PUPILS WITH SEND

CASE STUDY

Support for Huang, a Year 7 pupil

Huang has a diagnosis of ADHD and in particular struggles with staying focused during lessons for period of time. During primary school, Huang received High Quality Teaching and support in each of his lessons through adaptive teaching. Huang's teachers would use a combination of scaffolding support to keep Huang moving through tasks at pace, and hover support to direct him back on task, or change task. However, at times Huang was not making as much progress as his peers as he would leave a task to change focus.

As Huang moved to secondary school, his mum, Chen, was becoming increasingly worried about his progress in lessons. The change of lessons to different teachers meant that she was not able to keep track of how he was getting on as easily as when he was in primary school, and she was concerned that he may have gaps in what he was learning.

Chen contacted the school and an appointment was made with the Assistant SENCo. At the meeting the Assistant SENCo advised that as Huang was new to the school, they were in the process of gathering information from each of his lessons about how he was getting in, how he had settled in, and the progress he was making. It was acknowledged that the secondary school was a very different environment to the primary school that Huang had attended and that Huang may need further support.

The Assistant SENCo advised that they were looking at were there were gaps in Huang's knowledge and understanding in core subjects of English and maths, and what interventions would be most appropriate to start Huang on to close these gaps.

The Assistant SENCo also spoke about the Graduated Approach, and that now was the time to move Huang to this, so that information could be gathered about the challenges that Huang was facing, and that support and interventions could be reviewed. She stated that they were at stage 1, and a meeting in a few weeks' time would lead them into stage 2.

A date for a further meeting in four weeks' time was booked with the Assistant SENCo to talk through the findings and support that was to be implemented, and to develop the plan as outlined in the graduated approach (which is outlined in the next section).

THE SPECIAL EDUCATIONAL NEEDS REGISTER (SEN REGISTER)

Pupils who need additional support and are making less than expected progress are added to the SEN register. This is a register that each school holds to keep track of pupils requiring additional support. Pupils may be added to the register, or if they are making good progress and no longer need to be on the register, they can be removed. Adding and removing to and from the register can happen at any time and parents and carers must be informed by the class teacher or SENCo if their child is being added or removed.

When pupils are added to the register, the SENCo will have identified their main area of need, and this will be listed as per one of the four broad areas of need that are outlined in the Code of Practice (2015).

- ◆ Communication and interaction.
- ◆ Cognition and learning.
- ◆ Social, emotional and mental health difficulties.
- ◆ Sensory and/or physical needs.

For pupils on the SEND register, the assess-plan-do-review cycle as per the graduated approach will be followed, this is outlined now.

THE GRADUATED APPROACH

The graduated approach is used as a form of overarching assessment and gathering of information, to inform what is needed for a pupil when they need a different sort of approach to the majority of pupils in the class. It may be that they are moving from the bottom tier of support within the model in Figure 3.1 which includes a level of universal support including high quality teaching and what is ordinarily available to your child, to a targeted level of support in which specific interventions may need to be included.

The graduated approach is comprised of a four-part cycle: *assess, plan, do, review*. The cycle is worked through by the class teacher, in collaboration with the SENCo and with support and input from you as your child's parents and carers, and it also includes input from your child. The cycle ensures that by exploring the needs and challenges that your child faces in school, the right support for them can be identified, implemented and then reviewed and amended.

It is important to note, that at the centre of this approach is your child and your family, and gathering your views is vital in contributing, informing, and beginning this cycle.

In the past, the SENCo held responsibility for the management of all of the pupils with additional needs, however this has changed with the newest Code of Practice. So, it may be different from when you were at school yourself. The responsibility is now shared, and every member of school staff has an important role to play and responsibility to hold in the development, support, and progress of each pupil. The class teacher has more responsibility now and has the overview of each of their pupils with SEND within their class. They lead on the graduated approach for their pupils, and the review of any support plans that are in place for them.

As a parent or carer, your first discussion around your child should be with your child's class teacher. They can seek support from the SENCo, or if you would like further clarification, or if you are not happy with the support that your child is getting, then you can arrange an appointment with the SENCo. Sometimes the SENCo will hold the review meetings, and other times it will be the class teacher. This will depend upon the school, the number of

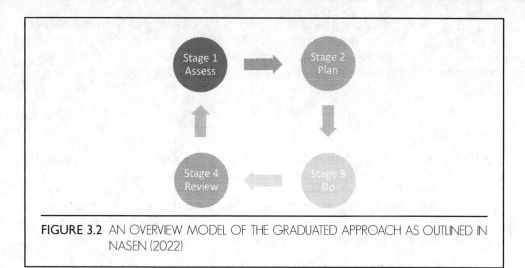

FIGURE 3.2 AN OVERVIEW MODEL OF THE GRADUATED APPROACH AS OUTLINED IN NASEN (2022)

SEND pupils at the school, and the experience of the SENCo and class teachers. It may be a mix, sometimes they hold the meetings together, and other times it will be one or the other. There is no definite way of who should be holding these meetings.

Let's outline the stages within the graduated approach.

Needs are not being met/class teacher has concerns:

Stage 1 - Assess

This initial stage includes gathering information from the daily types of formative assessment so that an overview of where the pupil has reached can be formed. It is the class teacher's responsibility to gather this information, it will include identification of any barriers that might be in the way of the pupil making progress that is in line with their peers.

The class teacher (and/or the SENCo) will have a discussion with the pupil and you as their parents or carers either on your own, or with the SENCo to establish your views on any challenges that your child may have. They will be looking for any gaps in knowledge, understanding or skills for your child, and whether any further assessments that the school can provide might be beneficial at this stage. The SENCo will also consider whether any referrals to other agencies or exploration of further external assessments might be useful.

Internal school assessments and tests might include: reading, spelling and maths tests; profiling tools for the assessment of speech and language challenges; communication assessments that may include looking at body language and responses to scenarios and behaviours, diagnostic assessments linked to Cognitive Abilities Tests (CATs) and the use of screening tools for the possibility of dyslexia or dyspraxia.

Your SENCo will arrange for any of these additional assessments to take place, and there may be a waiting list within your child's school for this, depending on who is conducting the assessments, their expertise, other pupils waiting to be assessed, and the workload of the person undertaking the assessment. Often these types of assessment are carried out by the SENCo themselves, or a specialist member of the support staff team that has had further training in the area and the implementation of the tool or test.

There may be restrictions on some types of assessment, for example, some dyslexia screening tools can only be used with pupils over the age of 7 or 8 years old.

REFLECT

Have you been invited in to school for a meeting to discuss your child? Did you discuss the challenges that they have at home, or the difficulties that you think that they are having in school? Often a child might open up to a parent about how they are feeling about school, rather than discussing this with a teacher, which is why it is important for school staff to have these meetings with you as their parent or carer rather than solely rely on your child's views. For example, one parent said:

> Jakob always wants to do his best and please everyone, so he gives the teach-
> er the answer he thinks they want to hear, if they ask him if he is ok, he will
> always say yes, even if he wants to run home and cry.

Is there anything you would want to let your child's school know about them at your next meeting?

Keep note of this as things easily get forgotten, keep a running list on your phone for example.

Stage 2 - Plan

At this stage, the information that was gathered in stage 1 is discussed and a plan formulated that will include support for your child based upon their emerging needs. The planning process will include everyone that is part of the support network for the pupil including your child themselves, you as their parents or carers, the class teacher, and the SENCo. If there are any external agencies involved in supporting the pupil, they will be included too.

Included within the plan, targets are set that are tightly focused around specific areas that have been identified. Each target should have action steps that will be granular and support the work towards the target. It will identify what the support is, who will implement this support, who will review it, and how and when it will take place. It will also include specific teaching strategies and any resources linked to this.

The plan will have a timeline with review dates set. The plan needs to be shared with everyone involved in working with the pupil, and this will include you as part of that team. If you are not included in a circulation list, ensure that you sit with your class teacher to read the plan together and to understand your role in working on the targets for any pupils you are working with. The plan may be presented as an Individual Education Plan (IEP), one plan, one-page profile, pupil passport or individual provision map. This will vary from school to school on how they choose to present this plan.

Stage 3 - Do

The responsibility of implementing the plan at this "do" stage is held with the class teacher. The implementation should be carried out on a daily basis and provision being implemented at all times. It could include strategies such as:

- High Quality Teaching
- Implementing specific individual strategies or interventions which might include one-to-one or group support in maths, English, communication or social skills.
- Directing staff to implement support or strategies such as working with the TA or LSA.
- Using formative assessment to monitor and review progress.
- Adjusting strategies in relation to progress made.
- Communicating with the SENCo, parents and carers with the progress being made.

Stage 4 - Review

The review stage is the final stage before the process is then repeated and the cycle begins again. A meeting is held in which you (and possibly your child) will attend and the targets are discussed and evaluated; where has progress been made? Have any further barriers been identified? It is an opportunity to reflect upon what is currently in place and what progress has been made.

These meetings are normally held separately and may be carried out by the SENCo, the class teacher, or a combination of both of them.

In preparation for the review stage, the class teacher, will gather evidence towards the targets to be used within the review. This might include considering thoughts and evidence on:

- Has the pupil achieved the targets set? Have they got any evidence to support this?
- If a pupil has not met a target, what progress has been made towards the target?
- Which interventions have been successful?
- What changes might need to be made?

At this point, it is decided whether your child has made enough progress to be taken off this graduated approach, or enters another cycle of: assess, plan, review, do.

YOUR CHILD'S VOICE IN THE GRADUATED APPROACH CYCLE

It is always important to gain the views of your child and to seek their input into their own development and support that they receive. Your child's voice will be a vital part of the graduated approach.

It is important for your child for many reasons including:

- Enhancing well-being and raising self-esteem.
- Demonstrating that their views are listened to and acted upon.
- Check that your child has a full understanding of their situation and have contributed to their next steps.
- Developing a collaborative environment.
- Ensuring that your child's individual needs are met by supporting them to identify what this means for them.

They may share their views before each review meeting to see how things are progressing. This could be through:

- A TA or LSA discussing their views with them and together completing a form or template to capture these views.
- Your child attending meetings and sharing their views in person verbally.
- The use of visual aids or prompts may be used in discussions and questions.
- Play based strategies may be used such as the use of a sand tray, play dough or puppets or dolls.
- Creative approaches could be used such as art work, or creating stories.

However, your child's views are gathered, it is important that they have a voice and contribute to their support and provision.

CASE STUDY

Pupil voice: Huang – From the Earlier Case Study

Linking back to the earlier case study with Huang, as part of the graduated approach, the views of Huang were really important to be heard and to be a part of the graduated approach to inform the next steps for Huang.

An LSA that was beginning to build a good relationship with Huang, held a meeting with him to discuss how he was feeling and how he was settling in to school. The LSA used a "my profile" template, which had areas on this such as what Huang thought he was doing well, what he would like help with, what other people would see in Huang and say that they liked about him.

Rather than give him the template to complete, the LSA used these areas as discussion points and noted down the responses from Huang. She knew that if she gave him the template directly, the writing element might put him off answering in any detail.

When Huang became distracted, the LSA gave Huang some paper and coloured pencils and asked him to draw what he thought an ideal lesson looked like, who was in it and what would they be doing. The LSA was then able to use this picture as a vehicle for the discussion.

If Huang had been a younger pupil, the LSA may have engaged him in sand play instead, drawing pictures in the sand, or through use of the puppets to role play what a good lesson looks like for him.

ASSESSMENT TOOLS IN SCHOOLS

There are many tools that are used to assess the needs of pupils in schools. They are mainly used by the SENCo, or someone that the SENCo is working with, to carry out and conduct the assessments such as a dedicated LSA who has been trained to administer them.

This section will give a brief overview of the types of assessment tools that might be used with your child, and what they are looking for. The tools are used to gain indications of the barriers to learning for your child, so that the appropriate strategies and support can be implemented.

- ◆ Assessment of Reading – This type of assessment analyses a pupil's reading skills including reading accuracy, the rate/speed of reading, fluency and comprehension, and understanding of the text being read. It identifies specific areas to work on, and provide interventions to target to bring about progress. It provides age equivalent scores.
- ◆ Vocabulary Scale – This assessment focuses on pupil's receptive vocabulary, what they are hearing, and what they understand from this. It can identify any issues or delays with vocabulary development in pupils from as young as 3 years old. It is a simple assessment in which a pupil selects from a range of pictures, which picture best represents what is being said to them.
- ◆ Dyslexia – There are a range of screening test for dyslexia on the market, and your school may have chosen a particular one for a reason. Some assessments are only suitable for pupils over the age of 7 or 8 years, and schools will have a rationale for why they choose particular assessments. The assessment tests measure working memory, integration memory, phonological processing and phonic decoding skills. It will give an indication of whether dyslexia is probable, but this is not a formal diagnosis.
- ◆ Dyscalculia – This assessment examines pupils' difficulty with numbers and arithmetic. It identifies pupils who struggle with maths, and furthermore identifies those with dyscalculia indicators. It also gives an age-related score.
- ◆ Recall – This assessment identifies cognitive difficulties related to memory. The tests examine the functions of working memory such as phonological loop; word recall, visuo-spatial, pattern recall and executive function; and counting recall. Age-related scores are also given for this.
- ◆ Reasoning – Non-verbal reasoning assessments focus on process and reasoning skills and can indicate future academic progress in areas such as maths and science. Verbal reasoning assessments focus on skills in verbal thinking such as vocabulary, analogies and logical reasoning.
- ◆ Developmental Language – This assessment looks at developmental language considering a pupil's understanding of vocabulary and grammar, and the pupil's replication and use of the features of language.
- ◆ Emotional Literacy – These assessments consider the areas of self-awareness, motivation, regulation, empathy and social skills. They are taken form the viewpoint of the pupil, teacher and parent or carer and then combined to gain an overall view.

✦ Mental Health – These assessment types look at the areas that will potentially have an impact on pupil's mental health such as: enjoyment, belonging, healthy living, resilience, distress, bereavement, and social aspects of behaviour. This will identify areas for further exploration with a pupil.

It is important to understand that the use of screening tools do not give a formal diagnosis. They do give an indication or probability of challenges that the pupil may have though, and this is enough to provide the right strategies to support the pupil, and evidence towards seeking access support for tests and exams.

EXTERNAL PROFESSIONAL ASSESSMENT TYPES LEADING TO DIAGNOSIS

If a parent or carer is seeking a formal diagnosis for Autism, ADHD or Dyslexia, then a pupil would generally need referring to a paediatric team. There tends to be very long waiting lists for assessments currently approximately 18 months. There are places which will conduct formal assessments privately that might lead to a diagnosis, but these can be expensive (around £2000 or more).

✦ Autism – The assessment carried out for children for Autism that is most commonly used in the UK is the Autism Diagnostic Observation Scheduled (ADOS) and is a series of assessments which includes observations of communication and social interaction, play and imagination. It is normally conducted by a team of professionals which may include a paediatrician, psychologist and speech and language therapist.
✦ Dyslexia – Formal dyslexia assessments are conducted by specialist teachers or psychologists. These must be conducted by and approved British Dyslexia Association (BDA) assessor to become a formal diagnosis.
✦ ADHD – Assessment conducted for ADHD is normally by a consultant psychiatrist.

THE ASSESSMENT PROCESS: SUMMATIVE ASSESSMENT POINTS

Alix (2020) outlines the formal summative assessment points throughout the education system. Summative assessment progress checks usually consist of a test or exam given at the end of a set piece of work, such as at the end of a half-term or school year. This includes SATs tests, GCSEs and A evels. They also include "teacher assessments", where a teacher rather than someone from outside the school is observing a child with a task or marking their work. The aim is to assess the level a child has reached at a given time.

Currently, these are the tests or assessments that are carried out in schools:

- In the Early Years Foundation Stage (Reception), two statutory assessments are carried out. Reception Baseline Assessment (RBA) and the Early Years Foundation Stage Profile (EYFSP). RBA considers children's starting points and is used to provide the department for Education with school-level progress measures. It is not used to label or track individual pupils. EYFSP is a statutory assessment of children's development at the end of the academic year in which children turn 5 and determines whether children have met Early Learning Goals set in the curriculum.
- In Key Stage 1 (Year 1), a phonics screening test is carried out. This is where children demonstrate whether they are able to "decode" words for reading is assessed.
- At the end of Key Stage 1 (Year 2), national tests (SATs) and teacher assessments are carried out in English, maths and science.
- At the end of Key Stage 2 (Year 6), national tests (SATs) and teacher assessments are carried out in English and maths, and also teacher assessments in science. Children aiming for a place at one of England's grammar schools take the 11-plus.
- At the end of Key Stage 4 (Year 11), GCSEs take place.
- At the end of Key Stage 5 (Year 13), A Levels, apprenticeships or post-16 qualifications are taken.
- In addition, pupils are often tested throughout the year and at the end of each school year by the school.

The government expectations are that pupils will achieve five GCSEs of grades 4-9 including English and maths. Pupils will be expected to gain a level 4 or above to be seen as meeting the national level of expectation set out by the Government. However, we know that this may not be realistic for your SEND child, and that exams may not be the best way to assess your child. This is what is currently in place though, and there are some ways to support your child through "Access Arrangements".

Access Arrangements

SEND pupils may need additional support in some form during exams and tests, and therefore they may need "access arrangements" to be implemented. To support giving them "access" to the test.

Access arrangements might be needed when a pupil has difficulty with reading or writing, have difficulty concentrating or have processing difficulties, have a hearing or visual impairment or have English as an Additional Language (EAL). As you can see from this list, many SEND pupils may need the additional support and access arrangements may need to be applied for.

TABLE 3.1 PUPIL SUMMATIVE ASSESSMENT STAGES AND AGES.

AGE	YEAR GROUP	STAGE	TESTS	CONSIDERATIONS
Birth–4	Nursery / Pre-school	Early Years Foundation Stage	Progress check (aged 2)	Apply for primary school place
4–5	Reception	Early Years Foundation Stage	Reception Baseline Assessment Early Years Foundation Stage Profile	
5–6 6–7	Year 1 Year 2	Key Stage 1	Phonics screening, National tests and tasks in numeracy and literacy - SATS	
7–8 8–9 9–10 10–11	Year 3 Year 4 Year 5 Year 6	Key Stage 2	National tests and tasks in Numeracy and Literacy SATS, possibly the eleven plus	Apply for a secondary school place
11–12 12–13 13–14	Year 7 Year 8 Year 9	Key Stage 3	School internal tests, termly or annually	Choose options for year 10 and 11
14–15 15-16	Year 10 Year 11	Key Stage 4	Mock exams, GCSEs or other vocational qualifications	Apply for sixth form, college or apprenticeship
16–17 17–18	Year 12 Year 13 (if at sixth form)		Mock exams, A levels Post-16 qualifications Apprenticeships	HE options and careers service
18 +			Undergraduate certificates, diplomas, degrees, HNC, HND, work-based qualifications	Careers service

When applying for access arrangements, a school will need to demonstrate that the pupil has a significant disadvantage to their peers without having the adjustment in place, and that the adjustments being applied for, are part of the pupil's normal way of working.

Pupils with an EHC plan automatically are entitled to an additional 25% of time being added on to SATs exams. Schools need to make an application for additional time for pupils without an EHC plan and for other types of support to the Standards and Testing Agency. Schools can only apply for support for a pupil that they would normally have the same support in class on a daily basis. Monitoring visits take place to ensure that this is the case.

For secondary school pupils for GCSEs and A Levels, schools need to apply to the Joint Council for Qualifications (JCQ) which oversee the arrangements for all of the examination boards for GCSEs and A Levels.

Types of support in addition to, or instead of additional time could include:

- The early opening of test packs so that papers can be adapted; papers can be opened one hour early and you would not need to apply for this, and this could be for: photocopying papers onto coloured paper, enhancing diagrams, enlarging text or preparing equipment. If additional time to the one hour was needed, this would need to be applied for
- Additional time to complete tests (outside that which can be given for pupils with an EHC plan)
- The use of a scribe
- The use of word processors or other technological devices
- Making transcripts
- Readers
- Accessibility objects in a maths test

Further guidance on applying for access arrangements and how support can be used is in the further reading section: DfE (2024) Key Stage 2 Access Arrangements Guidance, and the Good Schools Guide (2022).

It is important to note, that although pupils may receive access arrangements for exams, this might not be the case with course work too. As coursework is not timed, they are unlikely to gain additional time to complete coursework.

Below are some examples of pupils that have access arrangements in place.

CASE STUDY

From a Primary SENCo

Karim was dyslexic and in particular struggled with spelling and reading passages of text quickly. During class he would normally have additional support in writing through the use of word bank resources, referring to classroom displays, additional time and pre-teaching for new topics. As the Year 6 SATs approached, the class teacher made further use of the wall displays to support Karim in his learning, prompting him to actively use the displays for support and to visualise what was on them and how they would help him in his work.

Rather than sit the tests in the large hall with the other pupils, Karim stayed in the classroom where he was comfortable with his environment and felt more relaxed. The SENCo had applied for additional time (as Karim did not have an EHC plan) and he was granted an additional 25%.

Through staying within his familiar classroom, although the displays were covered, Karim could visualise what was on the displays and support him with remembering word structures, sentence starters and mathematical processes. This supported him to stay relaxed and recall the information that helped him. The additional time helped Karim to read the text in his own time and not feel rushed.

CASE STUDY

From a Secondary SENCo

Emilie has ADHD and had an IEP but not an EHC plan. Emilie generally coped well with school, but over the past year she had become more distracted and challenging in class. She was easily distracted by her peers during lessons, and she found it difficult to concentrate, needing frequent breaks during the lesson time. She had begun to fall further behind her peers through not being able to stay focused which had led to some behavioural difficulties and challenges for staff too.

Using the graduated approach of assess, plan, do and review, the SENCo and class teachers had been able to gather the views of Emilie, staff, and parents, and begin to plan further strategies to support her. Emilie had discussed how she felt; as though she needed to get up and move around more, this helped her to then refocus on the task, when she was redirected to do so. She said it also helped her to process the information or task and give her some thinking time.

Frequent planned breaks were built into Emilie's lessons, which gave her permission to move around, and leave the classroom if needed, this was supervised. This meant that Emilie stayed focused for longer as she knew that she had a planned break that was imminent, and this helped to settle the behavioural challenges that staff were facing.

As the GCSEs approached, additional time was requested and Emilie was allocated a further 25%. It was decided that Emilie would not sit her exams in the large hall with other pupils, but separately with a few other pupils in a nearby classroom. Planned breaks were built into each exam, and the papers were opened an hour before so that the breaks could be incorporated at appropriate time spaces in the paper, rather than in the middle of answering a question for example.

These adjustments enabled Emilie to take the exams, and the additional time supported her needing to take the breaks to manage her behaviour and impulses to continue and complete them.

CHAPTER SUMMARY

This chapter started by looking at the different types of assessment in schools and when these happen. It then goes into specific detail on how your child receives High Quality Teaching that may be adapted for their needs as part of ordinary classroom practice. This is followed by targeted support through interventions and more specialised provision. The chapter has a focus on the graduated approach: *assess, plan, do, review*, as this is so important in your child's support and progress. You and your child are directly involved in this approach cycle and your views and your child's views are an important part of this. The chapter also gives an overview of possible assessment tools that are used within schools that your child may undertake as part of the assessment process, and the processes for professional diagnosis and access arrangements.

The next chapter is going to look at the complex area of funding arrangements.

REFLECT

Think back on this chapter. What is your role in the graduated approach?

- How will you be contributing to this cycle?
- Is there anything that you are unsure of?

If so, speak with your child's class teacher, or create a list of questions to ask at your next meeting.

GLOSSARY OF KEY TERMS

- Adaptive Teaching – Scaffolded support for pupils to achieve the same aims, goals and objectives as all pupils.
- Formative assessment – Formative assessment happens on a daily basis and it forms part of you reviewing what you plan and teach your pupils.
- The Graduated Approach – The cycle of assessment for SEND needs; assess-plan-do-review
- High Quality Teaching – The current term used in schools to represent high quality teaching available to all pupils, and that is ordinarily available.
- Quality First Teaching – Quality First Teaching has been a popular term that has been used for several years within the education sector and by teaching staff. High quality teaching that is differentiated and personalised.
- Summative assessment – Summative assessment is a formal assessment of a block of work which happens at the end of a period or block of teaching, such as at the end of a half term or term, or a particular topic or unit of work.

FURTHER READING

- McPherson, R. (2022). *Neurodiversity: Why Exam Reform is Urgent*. TES.https://www.tes.com/magazine/analysis/general/neurodiversity-why-exam-reform-urgent
- The Good Schools Guide (2022). Access Arrangements. https://www.goodschools-guide.co.uk/special-educational-needs/your-rights/exam-access-arrangements
- Department for Education (DfE) (2024). Key Stage 2 Access Arrangements Guidance. https://www.gov.uk/government/publications/key-stage-2-tests-access-arrangements/2024-key-stage-2-access-arrangements-guidance

REFERENCES

Alix, S. (2020). *The Foster Carer's Handbook on Education; Getting the Best for Your Child*. CoramBAAF.

Department for Children, Schools and Families (DfCSF) (2008). Personalised Learning; A Practical Guide. https://dera.ioe.ac.uk/id/eprint/8447/7/00844-2008DOM-EN_Redacted.pdf

Department for Education (DfE) (2015). *Special Educational Needs and Disabilities Code of Practice; 0 to 25 Years*. DfE.

Education Endowment Foundation (EEF) (2022). High quality teaching. https://educationendowmentfoundation.org.uk/support-for-schools/school-planning-support/1-high-quality-teaching

National Association for Special Educational Needs (NASEN) (2022). *Teacher Handbook: SEND; Embedding Inclusive Practice (2022)*. Education Endowment Foundation (EEF). https://www.wholeschoolsend.org.uk/resources/teacher-handbook-send

CHAPTER 4

EDUCATION, HEALTH AND CARE PLANS

WHAT ARE THEY, HOW TO APPLY AND HOW TO APPEAL A DECISION

CHAPTER AIMS

✦ To know what an Education, Health and Care plan is.
✦ To know what an Education, Health and Care Needs Assessment (EHC needs assessment) is.
✦ To understand the role of the Local Authority (LA) in carrying out an EHC needs assessment.
✦ To understand the role of the LA in issuing an EHC plan, and then reviewing it.
✦ To understand the role of the SENCo in applying for an EHC needs assessment.
✦ To understand the role of the class teacher in applying for an ECH needs assessment.
✦ To understand the role of the SENCo in implementing the EHC plan and reviewing it.
✦ To understand the role of the teacher in implementing the EHC plan and then reviewing it.
✦ To understand how a parent or carer contributes to the EHC needs assessment and EHC plan.

INTRODUCTION

This chapter has the specific focus of supporting you to gain knowledge and understanding around Education, Health and Care plans. The chapter will outline what an EHC plan is, who it is for, and who can apply for one. It will look at the role of the school, and

DOI: 10.4324/9781032689159-6

the role of you as the parent or carer, and what routes you can go down when considering applying for an EHC plan.

The role of the class teacher, SENCo and the Local Authority (LA) will be looked at, and the legal requirements of the EHC plan. The chapter will conclude with exploring the implementation of the plan, what the plan looks like in practice within the classroom, and what the school should be doing to uphold their legal duties in relation to this plan.

There are five stages to an Education and Health Care (EHC) plan:

- Identifying the needs of children with SEND.
- Conducting an EHC needs assessment.
- Creating an Education, Health and Care plan.
- Implementing the final EHC plan.
- Regularly reviewing the EHC plan.

REFLECT

Jot down your thoughts around you own current understanding of EHC plans.

- What do you know about EHC plans?
- Does your child have an EHC plan?
- Are you considering applying for an EHC plan? If so, do you know the process for this?

This chapter should give you some deeper understanding regarding EHC plans, regardless of whether your child has an EHC plan in place already, or whether you have not even considered an EHC plan.

Firstly, the chapter will look at what an EHC plan is, and will then to progress to look at how to apply for one.

WHAT IS AN EDUCATION, HEALTH AND CARE PLAN?

An Education, Health and Care plan is a legal document which has been written by the LA in conjunction with reports and advice from specialists and professionals. The document is written for children and young people who are up to the age of 25 years old and who need more support than can be given under the provision outlined by a school and shown in the first two levels in Figure 3.1 in the previous chapter.

The EHC plan identifies and outlines the education, health and care needs of an individual and the support that will need to be implemented to meet those needs for that person. It identifies the outcomes that a child or young person would like to achieve. The plan will also identify the school that the pupil will attend, such as a local primary or secondary mainstream school, or a special school. This will only be agreed once a school has agreed to being able to meet a child's need with the support through the EHC plan.

Who Can Apply for an EHC Needs Assessment?

A request for an EHC needs assessment can be made by a young person themselves if they are aged between 16-25 years, or by anyone who thinks that the child or young person needs to have one. For example, a parent, carer, family member, a teacher, SENCo, doctor or health visitor, but this list is not limited. Most LAs have a form on their website that you can use to apply for an EHC needs assessment.

HOW LONG DOES AN EHC NEEDS ASSESSMENT TAKE TO HAPPEN, AND WHAT ARE THE STEPS INVOLVED?

The process should take no longer than 20 weeks from the submission of an application, through to a decision and the issuing of the final EHC plan. However, as many parents and schools will know, LAs do not have the money to fulfil their legal requirement. The lack of money from Government impacts on the LA to employ enough staff to fulfil this. There is an issue with the lack of Educational Psychologists (EPs) working in LAs, and further training to put more EPs through to where they are needed at the heart of SEND is very much needed. There are occasions were schools and parents have reported that the process has taken in excess of 40 or even 60 weeks.

Weeks 1-6

Once your application has been submitted, the LA have between 1-6 weeks to process your application and decide whether to proceed to an EHC needs assessment.

First an individual (parent or family member) or a school will submit an application to the LA for an EHC needs assessment. The LA will then review this application through a board or panel meeting, along with other applications, and they will decide whether your child's needs are already being met within the school that they are in, or whether, based upon the evidence that has been submitted, that your child's needs cannot be met with the level of support being offered in school, and therefore to proceed to an assessment of your child's needs.

At this point you will be notified of the outcome of this decision. If your application is declined, you will be able to appeal this decision, and the LA will provide information on how to do this within their decision letter. You will have two months to appeal, and if you do not appeal within this timeframe, you will not be able to appeal the decision, and will need to look at completing a further application with additional new evidence.

First, you will be invited to mediation with the LA, and you will need to attend this and receive a mediation certificate if an agreement cannot be reached. You will then attend a tribunal with The Special Educational Needs and Disability Tribunal (SENDIST) who consider parents' and carers' appeals against the decisions of the LA about children's special educational needs, where the parents cannot reach agreement with the LA.

If the LA agree to carry out an assessment, you will move to the next phase.

Weeks 6-12

In weeks 6-12, the LA will contact a range of professionals and yourselves and collect information from you all. Even though you may have submitted a great deal of information with the initial application, the LA will want to gather further information. This information will come from:

+ Yourself as the child's parents or carers.
+ Your child or young person, including their views, wishes and feelings.
+ The person who has submitted the request if it is not the parent, for example the school, or anyone in the list outlined in the previous section.
+ Staff in your child's current educational environment, for example the class teacher, SENCo or Headteacher.
+ A representative from social care, usually a social worker, if your child is working with one.
+ A health care representative, such as a paediatrician.
+ An Educational Psychologist (EP), who will normally visit your child and conduct an assessment and provide a report, even if one has recently taken place already.
+ Any other professional involved with the child that the LA thinks is appropriate.
+ Any person the child's parent or the child reasonably requests should be involved.

This process will take up to six weeks, and each of the individuals contacted will be given deadlines to return their information back to the LA. The LA will be wanting to see evidence that your child needs more support than a mainstream setting can normally provide for them. It will be wanting to see evidence of:

+ What sort of special educational need that your child has, it does not require a medical diagnosis.
+ The amount of help that your child needs, and why the school may not be able to provide this from their own resources and funding.

By week 12, the LA should decide whether they are going to be issuing an EHC plan. If the LA decided at this stage not to issue an EHC plan, then the parents must be notified with the information on the right to appeal and the process and outlined earlier with mediation and SENDIST.

Weeks 13-16

If the LA has decided to issue an EHC plan, then a draft version of this plan must be issued by week 14. This plan and all of the advice and reports that were written during this assessment phase will be sent to everyone who has contributed to the EHC needs assessment and to the parents or carer.

Once the parents have received this information, the parents have up to 15 days to respond to the draft version with any comments and changes that they would like to see happen, and to name their school of choice for their child. They can also request a meeting with the LA if they would like to discuss the EHC plan with them. As a parent, make sure that you do this if you any queries if they can't be answered on the phone or by email, or if you are unsure of anything.

When you have sent off your response regarding which school you are requesting for your child, then the LA consult with the school whether they can meet your child's needs. The school must respond within 15 days. A placement can only be refused relating to whether the enrolment of your child would affect the education of other pupils already at the school, or if the school does not represent the best use of the LA money. Sometimes a school will respond with requesting a higher banding for your child for additional funds to support them, or funding to support transition.

Weeks 17-20

At some point between weeks 17-20 the LA should issue the final version of the EHC plan. A copy of this will be sent to you, and to the school that has been named and that they will be attending. There will also be information on appealing if you are unhappy with the final plan that has been issued.

It is really important to note that this 20-week deadline is a legal deadline, and any extensions to this are exceptions and very rarely apply. As outlined earlier in this section, there is a lack of funding in LAs leading to this, and LAs are often short of staff due to staff shortages, or are chasing up responses from professionals (none of which are exceptions) and they try and delay this deadline. It is common for EHC plans to go beyond this time frame which against the legal deadline, and therefore do stand up for what are yours and your child's rights and complain if this happening. Your LA will have a complaints procedure to follow which will be on their website. This will be in stages via directly through the LA initially, and if you are not happy with the response received, then this can be escalated to the Ombudsman. There is a link to the Ombudsman in the "further reading" section of the chapter, which contains fact sheets to support you. We know that there are problems with the SEND system in this country through a lack of funding and staffing, but as parents we also need to demonstrate when problems are happening so that the scale of this can be noted, to ensure change.

Beyond 20 Weeks: Reviewing the Plan

Once your child's EHC plan has been received and it has been agreed and is being implemented, then this plan will be reviewed annually. For children under 5 years old, this will be every six months. Further detail on these reviews are coming up in the chapter.

TABLE 4.1 TABLE SHOWING A TIMELINE OF THE EHC NEEDS ASSESSMENT PROCESS FROM APPLICATION FOR AN ASSESSMENT TO THE ISSUING OF THE PLAN

WEEKS	LOCAL AUTHORITY ACTION
0	The EHC needs assessment application is submitted to the LA.
1-6	The local authority processes the application. Within six weeks of making the request, the parents will receive a letter from your local authority with a decision about the request for an EHC needs assessment. If the EHC needs assessment is submitted and accepted, the local authority will seek information from parents and professionals.
6-12	Those who are contacted for information related to the EHC needs assessment, have six weeks to respond. This is a legal requirement. The LA should decide whether or not to issue an EHC plan and reach this decision by week 12. By week 12 the Local Authority should decide if it will be able to start drafting the EHC plan.
13-16	If by week 12, the LA has decided to issue an EHC plan then it must issue the draft version by week 14, sending a copy to parents and all those who contributed to the EHC needs assessment. The parents have 15 days in which to respond to the draft with their comments and changes and to name the preferred school. Once the LA has received the parent's decision about the school placement, then they must consult with the school specified by the parents, and the school must respond with its decision within 15 days.
17-20	Between week 17 and week 20 the LA should issue the final EHC plan. A copy should be sent to the parents and to the school named in the EHC plan, where the pupil will be attending.
Beyond 20 weeks	The 20-week deadline is a legal deadline and any extension beyond the 20 weeks is limited to specific exceptions. The 20-week process is the maximum amount of time and the regulations say that decisions must be made as soon as is practicable, so sooner where possible.

ISSUES WITH GETTING THE RIGHT SCHOOL FOR YOUR CHILD NAMED ON THE EHC PLAN

Although you will request a particular school for your child, it might not be possible for your child to attend that school. For example, many special schools are very much over-subscribed. Although you can appeal to request a place, it might still not be possible if there is just not the physical space available. Work with your LA to find the best, most suitable school available for your child. You may need to consider transport for this, and further information on this will be in the next chapter when looking at funding.

In summary, the purpose of an EHC plan is to:

✦ Record the views, interests and aspirations of you the parents and your child.
✦ Provide a full description of your child's special educational needs and any health and social care needs.
✦ Establish outcomes across education, health and social care based on your child's needs and aspirations.
✦ Specify the provision required and how education, health and care services will work together to meet your child's needs, and support the achievement of the agreed outcomes.
✦ Enable you the parents to request a particular school or college.

Taking Care of Yourself during the Process

Applying for support for you child can be a lengthy and stressful process, and it is important to be mindful of the pressure and stress that this can cause. You want the best for your child, and you may be worried that they are not getting enough support at school, or making enough progress. The EHC needs assessment process can feel lengthy and you may have times where you don't hear anything, or you need to follow up with phone calls to see how the process is going (this is important to check it is on track in terms of timescales too). Ensure that you talk through this with family or friends when you are feeling the pressure or need support. You can talk to charities and seek advice and support from them, such as from SEND Family Support (link in the further reading section of the chapter), or via support that is offered through your "Local Offer" such as Information, Advice and Support Services (IASS) which is going to be explained in further detail later in this chapter.

CASE STUDY

A Parental Experience of Applying of an EHC Needs Assessment

Thea had concerns for how her son Xander was progressing in school. She was worried about how he might transition from the infant school to the junior school with the additional expectations and it being a larger environment. She also anticipated that these issues would become worse as he got older and wanted to ensure that he had the best support available as early on as possible, so that further learning was not lost for him, and he could make as much progress as he could.

Xander did not have an official diagnosis at this point, and he was waiting for further assessments, but the waiting time was lengthy. He had had just over a year of additional support from the school through interventions and time out of class with an LSA. He had also been attending a nurture group weekly.

Thea and her partner had many conversations around whether this was enough for Xander, and each time they concluded that they wanted the best for their child, and that this wasn't enough. They had met with the SENCo on two occasions at review points, and the SENCo had advised them that Xander was making some progress, and that they had many interventions in place. Xander did not demonstrate challenging behaviour in class and he was well managed by the staff. However, Thea believed that although this was the case, it did not mean that Xander was making enough progress and he still needed further support.

Thea arranged a meeting with the SENCo to discuss applying for an EHC needs assessment. The SENCo advised that she did not at this stage think that he needed it, as she thought his needs were being met in school, and that it was best to wait until he had transitioned to the junior school. Thea did not agree, and expressed that she would be making an application herself, as she did not want to delay the process.

Thea found the process difficult to navigate and challenging. First, she felt as though not having the support of the SENCo was detrimental to being able to ask her for support and guidance. Then, she found that not working in an education setting herself, the wording on the form was tricky to understand at times and she wasn't sure what evidence to present, for example, and whether it was enough. Finally, she struggled with writing about the worst elements of how Xander coped in in school at home. Everything that she seemed to need to express were all negatives, there were no opportunities to celebrate the positive elements of Xander.

After struggling with the initial stages of the process, she was advised by a local support group to seek some support from "Families in focus" which was a local charity that offered free support and guidance for parents of children with SEND. There are groups such as this located in each are, some of them are called families in focus, others have slightly different names.

Thea arranged a meeting, and she contacted a support worker who was volunteer and who had been through the process themselves previously. This really gave her a feeling of understanding and empathy towards her and what she was going through, and they had attended training on the processes that were in place. Thea's support worker helped her to complete the form and to submit the EHC needs assessment.

The assessment was not agreed at this first stage, and Thea took this to mediation with support from her families in focus volunteer support worker. It was then agreed that an EHC needs assessment would take place, with further evidence being sought from the school. However, an EHC plan was not agreed at this time.

Thea decided that she would not appeal at this stage, and maybe they should take the SENCo's advice and to see how Xander transitioned to the junior school. Xander continued to have challenges and he received a diagnosis of autism and ADHD when he was in Year 3. The new SENCo had been monitoring his progress carefully after a transition discussion with Thea, and where she was able to communicate her concerns. The new SENCo had been gathering further evidence on the challenges for Xander, and with the new evidence in addition to the previous evidence gathered by Thea, the SENCo and Thea worked collaboratively to submit an EHC needs assessment, which progressed to an EHC plan in Year 4 for Xander.

TOP TIPS

Progressing through the EHC Needs Assessment Process

- ✦ Gather as much evidence at the beginning of the process (it is easier
- ✦ the earlier you systematically collect and store these), whether you are submitting an application yourself, or through the school, retain medical reports, medication lists, and keep copies of these together. This will also be useful if you apply for Disability Living Allowance (DLA) or Personal Independent Payment (PIP) which will be explained in Chapter 5.
- ✦ Seek support from a local support group or charity to help with filling in your form.
- ✦ Make notes of dates so that you can track when the process has started, when you need to return information, and when to expect to hear from the LA.
- ✦ If a deadline passes and you were expecting to hear something from the LA but haven't, follow this up with them via phone call to ensure that the timeline is on track. If it isn't, ask for a clear expectation of when you will receive the information or progress to the next stage.
- ✦ On receiving the draft plan, check this thoroughly, and ask someone experienced to look at this with you, particularly section F. For example, are the targets SMART and clear? This will ensure that a school implements them in the way that you are expecting them to.
- ✦ If there are no places available at your chosen school, be open to explore other options, make school visits, and discuss these with your LA.
- ✦ Use the services available to you to discuss your thoughts, concerns, and options, such as the Information, Advice and Support Services (IASS) which is outlined later in the chapter.

> ✦ If you are unhappy with the process, timekeeping or support form the LA, follow this up through the appropriate complaint channels.
> ✦ If you are unhappy with the outcome of the EHC needs assessment, do seek mediation with the LA to see if an agreement can be made, or seek an appeal.
> ✦ Ensure that you take the time to celebrate your child's successes outside of this application process, as these can get lost in the process of demonstrating negative points.

One of the "top tips" above highlights the importance of targets being clear for the benefit of your child. The following case study outlines the difficulty when wording is unclear, or becomes amended without capturing the intended purpose.

CASE STUDY

From a Parent Regarding Their Child: Helena

Helena attends a mainstream secondary school, and she had recently received her EHC plan. As Helena's parents, we were originally happy with the targets that had been set, and through discussion it appeared that they were clear and understood by both the school and us.

One of the original targets set was:

If/when Helena is absent from a lesson, a summary of the work that was covered should be sent to Helena and her parents at the earliest opportunity, and on the same day that the lesson was implemented, to allow Helena time to become familiar with the work ahead of attending school the following day, and in readiness for the next lesson.

The school made some tweaks to the wording of this, to read:

Helena's teachers and the familiar adults working with her will be aware of the impact of missed learning and how it makes her feel about attending future lessons. She would benefit from any missed learning being shared with her to enable her to attend future lessons with confidence.

At the time, this seemed reasonable and clear. However, putting this into practice, we are now finding that the school has queried the timing of sending Helena missed work and she is not receiving the missed work before her next lesson, which is having a further detrimental impact on her confidence and learning. School have said that the EHC plan does not state the work has to be sent on the same day, therefore she is struggling to attend the follow up learning as she feels too anxious to go to the next lesson as she will not know what she is doing or what she has missed, and this is now beginning to escalate.

The revised target is not clear enough that Helena needs to have the work that has been missed before the following lesson, and we have been advised that we will now have to wait for the EHC plan review to rectify this and to make it clearer in the wording. Which is frustrating for us, and I think it will continue to have a detrimental impact on Helena, when the plan and targets should be supporting her instead.

WHAT DOES AN EHC PLAN LOOK LIKE?

There is no standard format for the plan, so there will be slight differences from LA to LA. However, every plan must have particular sections that are labelled in the following way so that all areas are covered, and the provision needed is set out clearly.

The sections needed are:

A: The views, interests and aspirations of you and your child.
B: Special Educational Needs (SEN).
C: Health needs related to SEN.
D: Social care needs related to SEN.
E: Outcomes – How the extra help will benefit the child
F: Special educational provision (support).
G: Health provision.
H: Social care provision.
I: Placement – Type and name of school or other institution
J: Personal budget arrangements.
K: Advice and information – A list of the information gathered during the EHC needs assessment.

As you will see, some of the sections correspond; The needs are outlined in section B, and the provision is outlined in section F, C and G are linked, and D and H are also linked.

APPLYING FOR AN EHC PLAN AS A PARENT

As a parent, you can apply for an EHC needs assessment, and you do not need a school to apply on your behalf or need the support of the school. However, a school would need to provide supporting evidence towards your child needing to have support above what they can provide as a school on an everyday basis, and the LA will contact the school for the relevant information as part of their assessment as outlined in the earlier sections. Often, it is the school that applies for the EHC needs assessment with the support of the parents as they will gather evidence that they have been collecting in school. However, you will have copies of support plans such as an Individual Education Plan (IEP) that have been implemented and reviewed, and if you do decide to submit an application as a parent, gather this evidence together.

You will also be asked to provide supporting documentation which could include any medical reports that you have previously received, any reports from professionals, or additional services that you have used to support your child. You will be asked to provide your concerns, and your thoughts around the provision needed for your child, and you will be asked to complete a questionnaire.

Once the application for an EHC needs assessment has been submitted, the correspondence will come to you directly as the parent. You will be advised whether an assessment will be taking place, and you will be notified of any key points and a timeline along the way.

THE ROLE OF THE SENCO - APPLYING FOR AN EHC NEEDS ASSESSMENT, IMPLEMENTING AND REVIEWING THE EHC PLAN

Application for an EHC Needs Assessment

The SENCo will decide in discussion with the class teacher and with you as parents that your child needs support beyond what is available, and what can be given with the current level of funding in school. As mentioned earlier, anyone can apply for an EHC needs assessment, but most commonly it is the pupil's educational setting such as the school, sometimes it is a parent, and occasionally it is another service or adult such as a family member. For this section, we are going to look at a school perspective.

A decision to apply for an EHC needs assessment may have been on-going for several months or even years. Evidence needs to be gathered over a period of time, and deciding when the school can no longer meet your child's needs, and when they will need further support, can be a tricky moment to judge, and sometimes all parties (the school and parents), may not agree on this timing. Either way, a range of evidence will be needed by a range of professionals. This evidence may include:

 ✦ The level of academic attainment, and the rate of progress that is being made by your child.
 ✦ The nature, extent and context of your child's needs.
 ✦ The interventions that have been put into place by the school already.
 ✦ Evidence of physical, emotional and social needs of your child.

✦ Evidence of working with external professionals, that their advice has been implemented and reviewed. For example, from an Educational Psychologist (EP), Speech and Language Therapist (SLT) and/or specialist teacher.
✦ That additional support and provision has been implemented beyond the SEN level of support expected by a school.
✦ That the request for additional provision will support your child to make increased progress.
✦ Several cycles of the assess-plan-do-review cycle as outlined in the graduated approach in Chapter 3 have taken place.

The SENCo will submit all of this information with the completed form to the LA, you will be asked for your views to accompany this request.

If the EHC needs assessment progresses to a an EHC plan, the school then decides how to use the provision based on what is in the EHC plan and what is outlined in section F of the plan, and how specific this is outlined. This may include direct and indirect work with a pupil.

The plan is reviewed annually, as mentioned earlier, but progress and targets will be reviewed more regularly. The SENCo will lead the review, and may or may not lead the interim review points, this may be an assistant, or a class teacher instead. Once the annual review has taken place, then the SENCo will send off the updated plan to the LA to approve this.

THE ROLE OF THE TEACHER – APPLYING FOR AN EHC NEEDS ASSESSMENT, IMPLEMENTING AND REVIEWING THE EHC PLAN

Application for an EHC Needs Assessment

The class teacher will support the SENCo when they gather their evidence ready to make an application for an EHC needs assessment. Robust recording of information throughout the graduated approach assess-plan-do-review cycles are needed. There should be at least two cycles of this, but often there may be more, which may span over more than a year. It is vital that the recording and storing of this information is well organised so that it can be retrieved, reviewed and collated when it is needed.

The SENCo will ask your child's class teacher for data on your child, evidence of the implementation of additional support and interventions, and the impact of these. This evidence will also be drawn from Individual Education Plans (IEPs) and the reviews from these.

The SENCo may also ask for the teacher to complete further check lists and questionnaires relating to your child, and they may also need to complete some of these with your child from their perspective.

Implementing and Reviewing an EHC Plan

Once an EHC plan has been issued for your child. The SENCo will work with the class teacher to look at the provision and support that has been set out in section F of the plan, and decide what this looks like in real terms within the classroom, or for the additional provision. The class teacher and the SENCo will work together to implement this provision.

FURTHER RESPONSIBILITIES OF THE LOCAL AUTHORITY

The LA must publish on their website something called the "Local Offer". This is a comprehensive list of all the support services that it expects will be available to children and their families. It must include what is available locally, and what is available outside of the local area but can be accessed by those children and their families within the LA. It should be more than just a directory of services, it should outline what is expected from the service.

ACTIVITY

Look up the "Local Offer" for your own Local Authority.

✦ What sort of services can they provide?
✦ How would you as a parent or a school access these services?
✦ What services are part of the LA geographical area, and what are out of area?

EHC plans must not stop because a pupil reaches the age of 19 years. Some may need longer in education to achieve targets and outcomes. In contrast some EHC plans will not need to stay in place until the age of 25 years.

Finally, LAs must provide Information, Advice and Support Services (IASS) to parents of SEN pupils, and this service must be provided free, be impartial and be confidential. Sometimes this service is run by a local charity rather than the LA themselves, and for other LAs, they run this service themselves.

CASE STUDY

The Case Study of a Primary School Pupil Progressing to an EHC Needs Assessment Application

Archie had coped well in infant school so far with the additional support that was in place, and because it was a large infant school, there was a substantial range of intervention programmes being implemented which Archie could join. These included:

- ✦ Anxiety support group/nurture group.
- ✦ One-to-one time with the school support dog, talking with him about feelings, and taking responsibility and care for another being.
- ✦ Social skills development group once a week.
- ✦ Playground support group, daily (or Lego therapy).
- ✦ Lego therapy (on days when not in the playground).
- ✦ Read, Write, Inc phonics programme, twice a week.
- ✦ Narrative group programme (alternating with the language support programme half termly, once a week).
- ✦ Language support programme.

The school were meeting his needs by going above and beyond what would normally be expected.

Archie's parents were becoming increasingly concerned with the struggles that Archie was having. They were worried about how he would cope when he moved up in to the junior school and expectations in terms of his learning increased. The SENCo, class teacher and parents met and agreed that it would be timely to consider putting in an application for an EHC needs assessment, so that the additional support that they felt would be needed, could be planned for. Archie had met with the paediatrician and was awaiting an assessment for autism and attention deficit hyperactivity disorder (ADHD).

The class teacher had been implementing Archie's Individual Education Plan (IEP) and had reviewed his targets at the end of term one. Targets for term two were being worked upon as part of the information gathering and assess-plan-do-review cycle. The class teacher had carried out the review meeting at the end of term one, and the next review meeting was due to take place. The teacher and SENCo gathered the evidence to demonstrate what progress Archie was making towards the targets, and what areas were still areas of difficulty for him. These include aspect of literacy, which Archie was attending interventions for, and challenges around Archie's Social, Emotional and Mental Health (SEMH) linked to his anxiety and sensory needs. The teacher discussed Archie's progress with the LSAs that were leading the support group sessions.

At the next meeting, the class teacher and SENCo shared with the parents their thoughts on the areas of need for Archie, and the information that they had collated. They advised the parents of the next steps, gaining the views of the parents and Archie, and arranging for an Educational Psychologist to visit and carry out assessments that would form as part of the application.

CASE STUDY

The Case Study of a Secondary School Pupil Progressing to an EHC Needs Assessment Application

Simone had a diagnosis of ADHD and demonstrated traits of Oppositional Defiance Disorder (ODD). She had been struggling with how she coped in mainstream education for several years. She often felt overwhelmed with the environment, the constant change, and she struggled to stay on task which often resulted in challenging behaviour seen in class, which led to arguments with class teachers, detentions and suspensions. Simone's parents and the SENCo were concerned that Simone may be at risk of receiving a permanent exclusion if behaviour continued in the way it was, and a meeting was called to discuss the next steps.

Simone was on a support plan through an IEP which was reviewed termly, but the staff, the SENCo and class teachers assessed that Simone needed further support that they were able to offer through levels 1 and 2 of the graduated approach.

A meeting was held with the parents, SENCo and Simone to discuss how the views of Simone and her parents would be gathered, and the SENCo would put together an application for an EHC needs assessment. The parents agreed to gather medical evidence in the form of letters and reports that had taken place for Simone, and to copy these for the school so that they could be included in the application pack.

Due to the escalating nature of Simone's behaviour, the parents also advised that they were going to request a paediatric review to look at Simone's medication. A reduced timetable for Simone was discussed so that small, positive steps could be made with what Simone was able to tolerate. She would also be attending the SEND hub rather mainstream classes.

Simone's parents felt relieved that they were had something to try and to progress to an EHC needs assessment to support Simone, as they were becoming increasingly stressed over how they could support her, and make the situation better. Thy had mentioned feeling helpless, but could now see a pathway forward.

INTERNAL EXCLUSIONS, SUSPENSIONS AND PERMANENT EXCLUSIONS

Sometimes challenging behaviour can lead to the exclusion of a pupil by the school. SEND pupils with an EHC plan are five times more likely to be excluded than pupils without an EHC plan. These figures do not include pupils with undiagnosed SEND needs. It is likely that a high proportion of these exclusions are due to the unmet needs of the SEND pupil, and the provision is not able to, or have the resources to support the pupil's needs. The pupil may need more of a specialist provision to meet these needs, but currently places and funding is in short supply.

There are three types of exclusions that a school can give a pupil: internal, suspension and permanent.

Internal Exclusion

An internal exclusion is when a pupil is removed from classroom activities for a fixed period of time, and is excluded from the normal daily classroom practice. They spend time somewhere else still on the school site, and they do not leave the school building.

Some pupils may exhibit challenging behaviour in order to go home as they struggle with the classroom environment. This approach means that they are then not rewarded for their challenging behaviour by being sent home to the environment that they want to be in, and doing things they prefer such as watching television or spending time on games consoles, and therefore reinforcing the negative behaviour.

Suspension

This is an external exclusion in which the pupil does not come to school for a fixed period of time, for example between one to three days. The school staff and parents then have a meeting on the return of the pupil to reintegrate them back into class, and to address the challenges that led to the exclusion.

Permanent Exclusion

A permanent exclusion may be implemented by the Headteacher when there are persistent breaches of the behaviour policy, or a one-off serious breach by a single incident. The permanent exclusion must be reviewed by a panel of the school governing body, and the parents or carers are invited to attend this. If the exclusion is upheld by the governing body, then the parents or carers have the right to appeal the decision by an independent panel.

At times, particularly when exclusions are used, there may be a breakdown of communication with pupils and parents or carers. It is important for schools to keep communication open and support parents or carers to find the best way forward to ensure the pupil is within the right provision to support their needs.

CHAPTER SUMMARY

This chapter has outlined what an Education, Health and Care plan (EHC plan) is, what it looks like, and how it is reviewed. It has discussed that an Education, Health and Care Needs Assessment (EHC needs assessment) happens first, before an EHC plan can be issued, and outlined the process and information needed for this to happen.

The role of the Local Authority (LA) has been explored, and the underpinning factor that the LA has a legal responsibility with the assessment of SEN pupils, and the issuing and implementation of an EHC plan. The role of the parent, the SENCo and the class teacher within the application process, the implementation of an EHC plan, and the review of it has been set out.

The next chapter will focus around the funding and support available to parents and to schools.

REFLECT

This chapter has looked at EHC plans and the process needed to apply for an EHC Needs Assessment for your child.

Reflect back on the chapter, is there anything you would like to look at in further detail? Or gain further clarification or understanding of?

If you didn't get the opportunity when you were reading through the chapter, make sure that you look up your LA "Local Offer" to explore the support available to you and your child.

GLOSSARY OF KEY TERMS

- Advice and Support Services (IASS) - A service for parents of SEN pupils run by the LA. This service is provided free, it is impartial, and it is confidential.
- Education and Health Care Needs Assessment (EHC needs assessment/EHCNA) - An assessment undertaken by the Local Authority (LA) to decide whether and EHC plan should be issued.
- Education and Health Care plan (EHC plan) - A legal document for children and young people aged up to the age of 25 years who need more support than is available through special educational needs support.

FURTHER READING

- Education Advocacy. https://educationadvocacy.co.uk/
- Gov.UK Children with Special Educational Needs and Disabilities. https://www.gov.uk/children-with-special-educational-needs/extra-SEN-help
- Independent Advisor of Special Education Advice (IPSEA). https://www.ipsea.org.uk/pages/category/education-health-and-care-plans
- Local Government and Social Care Ombudsman. https://www.lgo.org.uk/make-a-complaint/fact-sheets/education/special-educational-needs
- SEND Family Support. https://sendfs.co.uk/support/

CHAPTER 5

FUNDING AND SUPPORT FOR YOUR CHILD

CHAPTER AIMS:

✦ To gain an understanding of these different types of funding that may be available to a school for a child with SEND.
✦ To understand the types of funding that might be available to families of children with SEND, and how to access these.
✦ To gain an overview of the types of support and interventions that may be available in schools and how your child accesses these.

INTRODUCTION

Funding is a complex area within schools. There are different pots of money, and how it is allocated and spent can vary. This chapter will look at the core elements of funding relating to schools and your child, and it will look at additional pots of money that could potentially be accessed. The chapter will look at how this money could be used and spent on your child's needs, and there will be links to charities that you could approach to seek further support and funding for your child.

TYPES OF FUNDING

There are three levels of funding. I will lay this out in its simplest terms as it can get complex, there can be disputes over how funding is spent, and funding changes.

DOI: 10.4324/9781032689159-7

Per Pupil Funding

This is also known as level 1 (or element 1) funding:

This is money that is given by the government to every school for every child. It does not matter whether a child has SEND or not, the funding is given to the school per the number of pupils on the roll. This money should cover the cost of staffing and premises. The school does not have to apply for this funding, it is allocated to a school depending on the number of pupils on roll (the school register). It is around £7,000 per child, but varies between primary, secondary and special schools up to around £13,000 currently, but this changes year on year.

Notional SEND Budget

Also known as level 2 (or element 2) funding:

This funding is allocated for each pupil that needs SEND support and is on the school SEND register. A pupil does not need a formal diagnosis to be on the register and to receive this support, they need to have been identified as having additional educational needs. It is (at the time of writing this book) £6,000 per child. It is known as the Notional SEN budget. It is up to the school how to use this money, some schools will use it on staffing support, training or resources such as targeted interventions or equipment. The SEND Code of Practice states:

It is for schools, as part of their normal budget planning, to determine their approach to using their resources to support the progress of pupils with SEN. The SENCO, headteacher and governing body or proprietor should establish a clear picture of the resources that are available to the school. They should consider their strategic approach to meeting SEN in the context of the total resources available, including any resources targeted at groups particular, such as the pupil premium.

(CoP, 2015).

Element 3, "Top-Up" Funding and EHC Plan Funding and Banding

Also known as level 3 funding:

This is known as the High Needs Block or top-up funding, which is paid by the Local Authority or the Education and Skills Funding Agency. This is money allocated to meet the needs of an EHC plan. Depending upon the level of the EHC plan and the pupil's individual needs, then this amount can vary from several hundred pounds to many thousands of pounds depending on whether a pupil needs a specialist or residential placement. When your child is allocated a level of funding within their EHC plan, this is incorporating the level 2 funding of £6,000.

High Needs Block funding is given in levels, and recently has changed from numbered levels to lettered levels. Table 5.1 shows an example which replicates what LAs might outline, as the level of need associated with each banding level, and then a funding allocation is given to each of these banding levels by the LA. An example of this has been drawn from examples by different LAs and is outlined in Table 5.1.

Personal Budget

Previously the funding given to provision has solely been between the LA and the school. However, parents can now request for some of the funding to be given directly to them and for themselves to arrange a specific part of the provision. This gives you, as a parent, greater ownership and responsibility for the provision of your child if you want it.

If you want to request a personal budget, this must be done during the draft plan stage, or at an annual review and cannot be sought at any other time.

The budget can only be used for an element of provision that is outlined in the EHC plan, and the parents must outline why and how they are in a better position to provide and arrange this element of provision for their child. For example, the parents may already know and be working with a specialist teacher for their child, and they want them to continue providing weekly support or sessions for them.

The LA must outline to the parents the amount of the budget that will be allocated for this, what exactly the service is that they have agreed it can be used for, and any conditions that need to be met for the "direct payment" to be made to them or a young person if they are over the age of 16 years old.

The personal budget could be used for things such as:

◆ Carers to support the child in their own home.
◆ Activities in the local community such as clubs, sports and trips.
◆ Respite care.
◆ Equipment and resources that are not already provided by the NHS, and the maintenance of these if needed.
◆ Specialist teaching.
◆ Complimentary therapies.

The personal budget cannot be used for things such as:

◆ Anything related to the NHS or healthcare (this is provided by the NHS).
◆ Housing costs.
◆ Household bills.

The personal budget and direct payment of this are included within the main financial allocation that within the EHC plan, and it is not additional funding.

TABLE 5.1 AN EXAMPLE OF A SUMMARY OF NEEDS FOR EHC PLAN BANDING

BANDING LEVEL	BANDING DESCRIPTOR
Band A	Pupils at this level make slower than expected progress or who give some other cause for concern. Needs can be met by targeted adaptive teaching and highly focussed lesson design and modifying programmes of work. A pupil requiring this level of support will experience difficulties for which a mainstream school can address with support from within the graduated approach. Outside agencies will be involved if school-based interventions are not leading to the desired outcomes, and further specialist expertise may be needed, for example, Occupational Therapy, Child and Adolescent Mental Health Service (CAMHS), Speech and Language Therapist (SLT), Educational Psychologist (EP), and Specialist Teachers.
Band B	Pupils at this level can have their needs met in mainstream classes, predominantly working on modified curriculum tasks. This should include drawing on the specialist advice of services, or direct support by LA services and other agencies, as appropriate. The graduated approach has been implemented and will have included interventions recommended by outside agencies, but progress is not meeting the desired outcomes. In order to achieve the desired outcomes for the pupil, the school needs to access resources beyond that of the school through an Educational Health Care Plan. The EHC plan will support the school to provide opportunities for small group work based on identified need with opportunities for one-to-one support.
Band C	Pupils in this band will have an EHC plan. Pupils requiring this level of support will continue to make slower progress than expected and experience a moderate level of difficulties or a combination of moderate difficulties as outlined in Part II of this book. Pupils at this level will have attainments well below expected levels in all or most areas of the curriculum, despite appropriate interventions. They have much greater difficulty than their peers in acquiring basic literacy and numeracy skills and in understanding concepts. They may also have associated speech and language delay, low self-esteem, low levels of concentration and underdeveloped social skills. Pupils within this band may be described as having Moderate Learning Difficulties (MLD) or global, general or generalised learning difficulties.
Band D	Pupils in this band will have an EHC plan. Pupils will have substantial and/or significant difficulty in accessing the curriculum because of their identified needs. Pupils at this level may have attainments well below expected levels in some or all areas of the curriculum, despite appropriate interventions. They may have much greater difficulty than their peers in acquiring basic literacy and numeracy skills and will have greater difficulties than their peers in understanding concepts. They may also have associated speech and language delay disorder, low self-esteem, low levels of concentration and underdeveloped social skills. Pupils within this band may be described as having Moderate Learning Difficulties (MLD) or global, general or generalised learning difficulties.

(Continued)

BANDING LEVEL	BANDING DESCRIPTOR
Band E	Pupils in this band will have an EHC plan. It is expected that pupils requiring this level of support will experience a combination of substantial or severe difficulty in the areas of communication, cognitive development, behaviour, emotional well-being, physical difficulty and/or sensory impairment. They are likely to have significant cognitive impairments. They may also have associated difficulties in mobility and acquisition of self-help skills. All pupils requiring this level of support will require specialist provision. Pupils within this band may have Severe Learning Difficulties (SLD).
Band F	Pupils in this band will have an EHC plan. Pupils requiring support at this level will have a combination of substantial and severe difficulties in areas of communication, cognitive development, behaviour, emotional well-being, physical difficulty, or sensory impairment which significantly impacts on all areas of functioning both within and outside school. They are likely to have significant cognitive impairments. They may also have associated difficulties in mobility and acquisition of self-help skills. All children requiring this level of support will require specialist provision. Pupils within this band may have Severe Learning Difficulties (SLD). Most of these children will be educated within a specialist provision.
Band G	Pupils in this band will have an EHC plan. Band G level of support is for those pupils with special educational needs likely to be met by a highly specialist setting able to deal with profound and complex permanent needs. These are likely to arise from a combination of medical, primary care, learning, and communication, behavioural, physical, and sensory needs (including multi-sensory impairment). All pupils requiring support at this level will meet the requirements for specialist provision. Pupils will also have exceptional needs in the areas of behaviour, physical, medical or communication needs. For pupils requiring Band G level of support when behaviour is a concern, this will be extremely challenging for experienced and suitably trained staff. Where medical or physical needs are a particular concern, constant or a high level of monitoring and medical intervention will be required throughout the day. They are also likely to require full-time adult support to access all learning. Positive behaviour plans will require targeted and planned support from more than one adult for most of the day. Where communication is a concern, the pupil will rely on a trained adult to access a communication tool to communicate basic needs. Pupils who require Band G level of support may be described as having profound and multiple learning difficulties (PMLD). They are at a very early stage of development and need people around them who can help them to explore and interpret the world.

HOW THIS FUNDING MAY BE USED TO SUPPORT YOUR CHILD

You may believe that your child would benefit from full time one-to-one support by a Teaching Assistant (TA) or Learning Support Assistant (LSA), but this will really depend on your child's specific needs. It may be that they would benefit from one-to-one support all of the time, part of the school day, for transition times, or moving classrooms, or none of the time and that hover support or facilitation is best for them. Have a look at what provision is specified within your child's EHC plan. Does it specifically say that your child needs one-to-one support?

The EHC plan funding includes the already allocated £6,000 of funding awarded within element 2, so do not be mistaken that the amount stated within your child's plan is in addition to this. You may think that your school is getting more than they do. Also look at the funding, and consider how much one-to-one support would cost, for a member of staff to work solely with your child all week? Is this the best use of the funding? Some of this funding will need to be spent on staff training, for example, all staff need training in SEND, and I think everyone would agree how vital this is. TAs and LSAs never have a great deal of time for training, but making sure that they have relevant training in SEND and areas of your child's need is absolutely vital so that they can provide the best support and understanding for your child.

Your child may also benefit from specific interventions; these may or may not be outlined in their EHC plan, or it may be implied that they would benefit from support in a particular area, and the school may deem an intervention the most suitable way to deliver this. Some interventions will need funding to buy the intervention programme itself, which may be an online programme, or a member of staff may need to attend training on the programme, or specific resources may need to be bought in relation to the programme delivery.

As you will see, the complexity of how the funding is spent increases when each of these factors is considered.

CASE STUDY

From a Parent That Has Just Received and Agreed to Their Child's Final EHC Plan

I was really grateful that Freddie received his final plan, it felt a huge relief and weight had been lifted from my shoulders. I thought that it would solve all of the school issues that Freddie and his school were experiencing. However, I didn't really know or understand what this meant in practical terms. I thought that Freddie would now receive one-to-one support, and would have someone with him all the time to help him manage his behaviour or to take him out of the classroom. So, when this wasn't happening, and there were still issues occurring, I felt quite angry and upset! I had a good grumble about the school and wrote a complaint to the SENCo. The SENCo invited me in for a discussion, and I am really glad that I had this opportunity for her to explain to me what the EHC plan looked like in reality within school, and why the school was choosing to implement it in this way. I really had no idea before this!

The SENCo advised me that they had been allocated a small amount of money for Freddie, that really didn't cover a full-time one-to-one for him, and actually it wasn't the best way to support him anyway. Freddie was in Year 8 at secondary school, and for him to be seen with a member of staff all the time may not be what Freddie was comfortable with, he needed support to develop independence, and what was really needed was for Freddie to be supported at times when he needed it, when he was feeling as though he wasn't coping with his emotions, and support to help him deal with this.

The SENCo outlined how the funding was being used to support Freddie, which included an LSA being available to check in on Freddie at the end of the lessons and support him moving between classes and settling in to the next class. Freddie was also receiving an intervention involving managing his emotions and dealing with anger when things didn't go as planned or how he wanted them to. This was being delivered to him twice a week over an eight-week period. I came away from the meeting feeling much happier that I understood what was in place and why. I thought that maybe a meeting with the school when the EHC draft plan was issued may have been beneficial to help me understand what this meant in real terms within school, so that if I had wanted to question this at the draft stage, then I could have done, but I didn't really know or understand the process. However, the meeting with the SENCo was very useful, and I also understood that we could review Freddie's targets and provision if we didn't think it was working effectively for him.

REFLECT

If your child has an EHC plan, reflect on the following:

◆ Do you know what funding goes to your child's school?
◆ Do you understand how this is spent?
◆ Are you happy with how your child is being supported and the provision that is in place for them?

If the answer is no to any of these questions, arrange a meeting (or at the next review meeting) with your child's class teacher or SENCo and ask them to talk you through this.

INDIVIDUAL PUPIL RESOURCING AGREEMENT (IPRA) FUNDING

Individual Pupil Resourcing Agreement (IPRA) funding is provided by Essex County Council, but do explore with your LA to see what funding they offer that might be similar to this, or called something different.

Schools can apply for IPRA funding and it is normally awarded for up to one year, but it can be reviewed on an annual basis and continued for more than a year. If a school is claiming medical IPRA for a pupil, then it can be claimed on a longer-term basis if medical needs apply.

IPRA funding can be given to schools without the need for a statutory assessment of any kind. It will be awarded for specific circumstances such as:

- Medical needs funding:
  Pupil has no significant SEN but requires additional resourcing to support medical needs.
- Transitional funding:
  Pupils transitioning from Nursery / Preschool to Reception, KS1 to KS2 (if from an Infant school) or those transitioning from KS2 into KS3.
- Pupils arriving into the LA from another LA with significant SEN and no EHCP in place.

IPRA should not be regarded purely as a means of receiving additional/early funding to enable schools to collate information to support a request for a statutory assessment.

TRANSPORT

Most LAs will state that they will only provide transport for a child to the "nearest suitable school". So, if you want to send your child to another school because you believe that it would suit their needs better or provide for them better, then the LA may not pay for transport costs or provide transport for your child if it is further away than another school that they believe could provide for your child.

This can be frustrating for parents because you know your child and will have taken the time to view schools and see what school is best for your child.

The LA may agree to name the school of your choice on the EHC plan, but with the condition that you as parents will pay the costs of the home to school transport. It is common for LAs to ask for parents to sign a form that they agree to this, and that they will be paying the costs for this and that there is no requirement or obligation for the LA to pay transport costs.

Professional Discussion

If your LA state that they will name your school of choice only if you agree to pay for the transport costs, ask the LA and find out the answers to the following questions:

- What is the difference in transport costs, from the LA suggested school (the nearest one to home that they believe meets your child's needs) and your school of choice?
- Is the difference in cost relatively low?
- If they haven't investigated the difference in costs, it is worth finding this out for yourself.

> ◈ Can you find a cheaper transport arrangement, and ask for a personal budget to cover the costs?
>
> The LA must have carried out this investigation of costs *before legally* relieving themselves of the duty to pay for transport costs.
>
> *This is something that could be explored at a tribunal if the LA is requesting to name both the closest school and your choice on the EHC plan.*
>
> Remember this is about the most efficient use of resources. A tribunal will look at this and decide whether it is, and to agree to name solely your school of choice, or to agree with the LA and to list both schools, so that you can decide whether or not to choose your school of choice and agree to pay for transport, or to agree to the nearest school.

Travel Training

Travel for SEND pupils can be extremely stressful and anxiety-inducing. This can be whether they are getting transport to and from a local school or college, for example by bus, train, shared taxi or taxi on their own. Or whether they have to travel further afield to a school that is suitable for them which could be some distance away, and your child may be on transport for over an hour each way.

Some LAs will offer support for travel training. Look this up on your LAs "Local Offer", and see whether this is something that would support your child in developing the skills to travel to a known destination. Some LAs offer this free of charge for a child with an EHC plan, for others, for there will be a cost involved.

Travel training involves a support worker, working with your child or young person to plan their route, and support them on their route until they are confident enough to do this themselves and cope with any unexpected changes.

Wider Travel

There is further support for wider travel beyond going to and from school or college too. You could apply for a disabled person's bus pass, which will give a carer free or discounted travel if they are with a person (your child) that has one of these passes.

There is a similar scheme for people holding a disabled person's railcard, in which the holder of the card can get a third off rail fare for themselves and someone who is travelling with them.

DISABILITY LIVING ALLOWANCE (DLA)

Your child does not need a diagnosis to apply for Disability Living Allowance (DLA).

To apply for DLA for your child, your child will need to be under 16 years old, and need extra looking after than a child without disabilities, or needing extra care, or they have difficulty in getting around when you compare them with other children of the same age. To apply for DLA, your child must have had these difficulties for at least three months, and you will be expecting them to have them for at least another six months.

DLA consists of two parts: a care component and a mobility component.

Care Component

Each component has different rates depending on the level of care that your child needs. The rate your child gets depends on this level, for example:

✦ lowest rate - Help for some of the day
✦ middle rate - Frequent help or constant supervision during the day, supervision at night.
✦ highest rate - Help or supervision throughout both day and night.

Mobility Component

The rate your child gets depends on the level of help they need getting about, for example:

✦ lowest rate - They can walk but need help and or supervision when outdoors.
✦ highest rate - They cannot walk, can only walk a short distance without severe discomfort, could become very ill if they try to walk or they're blind or severely sight impaired.

There are also age limits to receiving the mobility component:

✦ lowest rate - The child must be 5 years or over.
✦ highest rate - The child must be 3 years or over.

(Government, 2023)

To claim DLA, you need to be the parent or carer of a child, or look after them as if you are their parent; for example, this includes grandparents, step-parents, guardians, foster-carers and siblings. The form is quite long, but it is worth applying for, so do seek support when making an application if you find this overwhelming. Parents do not know about applying for PIP and can miss out on years of potential payments and financial support for their child.

When your child reaches the age of 16 years, DLA will stop and you will need to claim Personal Independence Payment (PIP) instead. You will be notified by the government that this will need to happen. PIP is outlined in the next section.

PERSONAL INDEPENDENCE PAYMENT (PIP)

Your child or young person can gain Personal Independence payment if they are within the following categories:

* They are 16 or over.
* They have a long-term physical or mental health condition or disability.
* They have difficulty doing everyday tasks or getting around.
* You expect the difficulties to last for at least 12 months from when they started.

You will receive a letter stating that your child's DLA is due to stop and they will need to apply for PIP. This can be a worrying time for both you and your child. You might decide that your child is not able to take responsibility for their own finance at the age of 16 year, and it will be likely that they are still living with you and they are receiving a great deal of support. This is fine, and when you receive the application, you will be given the option to continue to have control of their finances and payments of you believe that they are not able to do this for themselves at this time.

You will receive a letter shortly after your child's 16th birthday, and you will need to apply for PIP, otherwise their DLA will stop. While you are going through the application process for PIP, your DLA payments will continue.

Once your child has been awarded PIP, the payments may change; they may be awarded a different level of payment than what they were receiving when they were awarded DLA.

You can get PIP on top of Employment and Support Allowance or other benefits. Your child's income, savings, and whether they are a young person who is working or not, do not affect their eligibility.

Similar to DLA, PIP has two components: a daily living part, and a mobility element. These components consist of, if you need help with:

Daily living part:

* preparing food.
* eating and drinking.
* managing your medicines or treatments.
* washing and bathing.
* using the toilet.
* dressing and undressing.
* reading.

✦ managing your money.
✦ socialising and being around other people.
✦ talking, listening and understanding.

Mobility part:

✦ working out a route and following it.
✦ physically moving around.
✦ leaving your home.

Your child does not have to have a physical disability to be awarded the mobility part. They might also be eligible if they have difficulty getting around because of anxiety.

(Government, 2023).

The Government Department for Work and Pensions (DWP) will assess how difficult your child finds daily living and mobility tasks. For each task they'll look at:

✦ whether they can do it safely.
✦ how long it takes them.
✦ how often their condition affects this activity.
✦ whether they need help to do it, from a person or using extra equipment.

Your child's carer could get carer's allowance if they have caring needs, which is outlined in the next section.

(Government, 2023).

As with DLA, the form can be long and overwhelming; again, seek support to complete this. It is a good idea to collect as much information as you can and send this in. Your child (with support) may be asked to attend a centre for assessment or a telephone assessment. Remember that you can take responsibility for this element. If enough information and evidence are sent with the application, then this may not be required at all.

CARERS ALLOWANCE

You or a member of your family may do a significant amount of caring for your child, beyond what is normally expected for a child or young person of their age. If so, you or they may be able to apply for carer's allowance. The person applying does not have to be related to, or live with your child. Only one person is allowed to claim an allowance for your child.

Carer's allowance can affect other benefits that you and your child might get, so do look at this carefully.

Information on DLA, PIP and Carer's allowance and guidance on how to apply for these can be found on the Government website (Government, 2023).

CASE STUDY

From a Parent Transitioning From Claiming DLA to Claiming PIP

When Maya was 7 years old, someone at our parenting group suggested that I could be claiming DLA for Maya. I hadn't heard of this before, and hadn't realised I could be getting some additional financial support for them. No one had told me or advised me of this, which was a bit frustrating as we could have been claiming this earlier; instead, we had been struggling to find the additional money to try and keep consistent caring in place for her. I went through the process of claiming, and I was surprised by how much support I gained for her. I was awarded some money for both the care and mobility components for Maya.

At this point we did not have a formal diagnosis of any particular needs, although we suspected that Maya was autistic and she had a high level of anxiety. The funding awarded for DLA greatly supported us in providing consistency in care for Maya. Due to us working as parents, it was difficult to provide the consistency of care that Maya needed before and after school, which created further anxiety for her, and we were able to use this money to provide care at school with adults that she knew, and for her to attend enrichment clubs.

Naturally I began to get anxious myself when Maya approached 16 years old. She had developed so much, and some things she was able to cope with, but other challenges and issues that she had just got bigger. Her anxiety had soared, and she needed mental health support through her school and through CAMHs, she found it difficult to be in busy spaces, and she was unable to use any sort of transport. At this point, she had gained her Autism diagnosis (when she was 9 years old), and general anxiety was outlined within this.

Over the years I had kept a file with all of her paperwork in, her diagnosis report, her EHC plan application and plan itself, all the school reports and plans, the application for her blue badge, and records from her mental health support. I was very glad that I had been doing this, as it was easy to locate the supporting evidence for the application.

As we drew close to Maya's 16th birthday, I received the letter to say that we would need to put in a claim. It also stated that if I believed that Maya was unable to take responsibility for this payment, I could outline why and ask for this payment to come to myself. I did this, and this was straightforward to put into action. A further letter came through just after her 16th birthday, and I needed to call up a number and say that we wanted to apply, the call lasted about 15 minutes, and it was basic questions around the practical elements of applying, confirming Maya's national insurance number, for example. We then received the pack in the post.

The pack was daunting! There were a lot of questions asking for examples and evidence around each of the areas. But, I was able to answer them using the evidence that I had. I took my time and went back to add to them over the course of a week so that I didn't forget anything that I thought may be relevant.

I received a postal reminder of the deadline, but I sent off the form and the evidence in plenty of time. Around a week later, I received a text to say that they had received my application and were reviewing this. At this stage, one of three things could then happen;

1. Maya could be awarded PIP based on the application and evidence.
2. We may receive a phone call assessment to follow up on the information given.
3. We may be asked to attend an in-person assessment.

For Maya, we received a phone call to clarify and be asked several questions around some of the areas and questions. The call lasted about 45 minutes and Maya did not speak during this time, I answered the questions on her behalf, and the assessor was fine with this. I ensured that I had a copy of my application with me and any further notes and evidence so I could refer to these. It was very stressful for me, but it went ok, and the assessor was very good and patient with me. After this, I waited around six weeks for a decision (while still receiving DLA), and then I received a letter outlining Maya's award for PIP, and the scheduled payments.

I do worry how Maya will cope in the future if she ever needs to try and apply for this herself, I know it just wouldn't be possible, she will always need some support to do this to ensure that she is able to get all of this information across.

TOP TIPS

Tips From Maya's Mum in Transferring From DLA to PIP

+ First, explore all the benefits that you may be able to claim for your child. Seek support from charities or parent support groups so that you don't miss out on anything that you may be entitled to, to support your child.
+ Keep good records for your child's needs. Any reports, appointments, support plans, etc., so that you have them when you need them.
+ Make notes on things that you remember your child has difficulty with. Keep a record of this over six months prior to them transitioning to DLA. You will be surprised by the number of things that you may forget. For example, all of their care needs, around cooking, bathing, reminding them, or supporting or prompting them to wash their hair, or needing to cut their toenails for them.
+ Take your time to complete the form, it is lengthy, split it into sections and complete a chunk at a time, but then go back to this after a few days once you have had the chance to reflect on this and add to it if needed.
+ Ask for support and advice from parent groups, or have someone to look over your form to see if you have missed anything.
+ There are lots of Facebook groups and TikTok post on supporting an application for PIP, these offer useful advice too if you are on any of these platforms.

CHARITIES

Some charities will offer support through grants for equipment for a SEND child. It is worthwhile looking at these charities if you are on a low-income budget. For example, look at the Family Fund and Disability Grants which have links in the "Further Reading" section at the end of the chapter.

CHAPTER SUMMARY

This chapter has had a focus on the funding and financial elements of support for your child. The first section of the chapter looked at how funding in schools works. It is not straightforward, and how this money is used and allocated within school is complex and dependent on how the individual school decided on it's use. For example, it may be that your child does not receive one-to-one support as you might expect because it might not be the best type of support for them, or funds may be allocated for resources or training.

The chapter also looks at potential other sources of funding that your school may be able to claim, and for transport to and from school. The final sections of the chapter give an overview of what you can personally claim to support your child such as DLA, PIP and carer's allowance. There are links to further supportive reading around charities and how they may also be able to support by providing additional resources or equipment for your child.

REFLECT

This chapter has looked at funding elements that could be available to support your child. Is there any area that you would like to explore further such as approaching a charity for support for equipment or resources, or seeking some personal funding for your child such as DLA or PIP?

FURTHER READING

- Disability grants. https://www.disability-grants.org/grants-for-children.html
- Education Advocacy. https://educationadvocacy.co.uk/
- Family Fund. https://www.familyfund.org.uk/
- Home to school transport myths. https://councilfordisabledchildren.org.uk/sites/default/files/uploads/files/top-home-to-school-transport-myths.pdf
- Special educational Needs Transport Advocacy Service (SENTAS). https://sentas.co.uk/

REFERENCES

Education Advocacy. https://educationadvocacy.co.uk/

Government (2023a). Carer's Allowance. https://www.gov.uk/carers-allowance

Government (2023b). Disability Living Allowance (DLA). https://www.gov.uk/disability -living-allowance-children

Government (2023c). Personal Independence Payment (PIP). https://www.gov.uk/pip

PART III

LOOKING FORWARD

CHAPTER 6

TRANSITIONS

FROM EARLY YEARS TO POST-16 AND BEYOND

CHAPTER AIMS

✦ To gain an understanding of the main transition points in educational settings.
✦ To examine the challenges that children and parents and carers may face during these transition points.
✦ To consider the options and opportunities that children and parents and carers will have during these transition points.

INTRODUCTION

This chapter focuses on the challenges and opportunities at the transition points in your child's education. Whether it is moving into their first formal education setting, or moving on beyond compulsory school age, the chapter will explore all of these age ranges and stages in your child's development.

As a parent, you will face many questions and considerations for your child as they progress through the stages, which can be quite stressful. This chapter will support you with answering these questions and asking further questions to support your child as they work through their educational key points.

It is important to note that the compulsory school age for your child is the September after they turn 5 years old. However, you have the right to send your child to school full-time from the September after they turn 4 years old.

DOI: 10.4324/9781032689159-9

TRANSITIONING INTO AN EARLY YEARS (EY) SETTING

For some parents the decision when to send their child into their first educational setting can be very difficult. You may have spent considerable time at home with your baby or small child and deciding when is the best time to move them into an Early Years (EY) setting, and for how long each week they should be going can be a difficult decision. For others, working may dictate these decisions, and the need to go back to work ensures that you must place them into an EY setting.

At this time, you may have a clear understanding of your child's additional needs, but you may not. You may know that they have additional needs, but at this point, not be able to define what they are, or what they will be when they move into a formal educational setting.

First, let's explore the different types of EY settings that your child could possibly attend.

Pre-School

A pre-school is an early years' setting for children that are aged between 2 and 5 years old. Children in this setting will be placed in a semi-structured environment following the early years foundation stage (EYFS) which is the framework before the national curriculum is followed in school. This will support children to transition to a reception class.

Sometimes pre-schools are held in community halls, or church buildings, or they are attached to primary schools. Those that are attached to primary schools are normally open term-time only and closed for the school holidays just like a school. Most of these pre-schools are open from 9am–3pm, similar to the school day too. It is likely that your child would attend for morning or afternoon sessions, which would mean a two-and-a-half to three-hour session each day.

Pre-schools may offer wrap-around care too, such as breakfast clubs or after-session clubs and holiday schemes. As pre-school isn't compulsory, pre-schools will take children from the age of 3 of 4 years old. The benefits to your child for placing them in a pre-school are that it will support your child to build social skills, concentration, confidence and communication skills.

Day Nursery

Some day nurseries may be privately run, others by the LA, but they will all be Ofsted registered. The main difference between a nursery and pre-school is that a nursery is set up to take babies as young as 6 weeks old, right up to children at the age of 5 years old. Nurseries will offer the education element that pre-schools do and they will also follow the

EY framework, but they will offer additional benefits such as the extra childcare that might be needed. Often nurseries are open from 7 am to 7pm each day, and throughout school holiday times.

Because a nursery has your child for this extended period of time beyond that of a pre-school, it may provide breakfast, lunch and tea, and offer further enrichment activities such as forest and beach school sessions, music and movement classes, a language class and yoga.

Your child will be assigned a key person who will get to know them and you, and your child will be placed in a room or area of the nursery which has been designed for the needs of children similar in age to your own child.

Children's Centres

A children's centre may offer childcare in some form of a pre-school, and they often have a further range of support for parents and families of children under the age of 5 years old.

Child Minder

A registered childminder is a self-employed person who looks after your child in their own home. They are regulated, and will be registered with the LA and Ofsted, and some with an agency. Some childminders may look after children all day, or they may look after them before and after another educational provision such as pre-school or school.

Childminders will do a range of activities with your child, including planning and preparing meals, and providing learning activities. Childminders will also plan and set out their activities in line with the statutory EYFS framework.

Early Years Considerations

It is important to note that all settings must follow the EYFS statutory framework and they are Ofsted registered. The main differences are the size of the setting, the length of the sessions offered and the accommodation where the setting will run from. These are the elements that you will need to consider. All settings will have a SENCo (they most likely will not have QTS), the childminder will fulfil this role themselves for the children in their care.

When considering which setting will be best for your own child, you will need to ask many questions.

Consider your child's needs as best as you can, as there will be many unknowns at this stage as they progress to spending time away from you. You might need to consider the setting's location; how far do you want to travel? The size of the setting, larger settings may have more resources, equipment and provision, but a smaller setting may be quieter and more manageable for your child.

REFLECT

If you have a young child that you are considering an EY setting for, think of the following questions to ask yourself and the setting:

+ What is your child's current needs?
+ What kind of care and education do you want your child to have at this stage?
+ What are the costs involved?
+ How many other children will your child be with? What is the ratio of a keyworker to children?
+ What would a typical day look like for your child?
+ What resources may they have that will specifically support your child's needs?
+ How do they deal with children that are showing challenging behaviour?
+ How do they support toilet training?
+ Is there an Early Years SENCo that is employed by them? You might need this as you move through this first phase of education.

When you begin to look at what type of EY provision you would like for your child, it is good to explore the settings and to see which one might support your child the best. Think back to Chapter 1, there was a case study of Maria and Antonio, in which Maria was considering secondary schools for her son.

Do you remember the *Top Tips* form Maria? They are applicable across each time your child makes an educational transition. Let's recap on some of them here now, but apply them to this stage:

TOP TIPS FROM MARIA

1. Ensure that you arrange visits at the local EY settings for your child, consider all of the settings, even if you have children, or previous children have attended one, think of them as individuals. One setting may support your child differently to other settings and children.
2. Speak with a SENCo of the setting if they have one, and ask them for real examples of how your child might be supported.
3. Keep an open mind to the different settings, do not listen to what others say, each setting is different for each child, make your own visits and make your own mind up as to which setting will be best for your child, remember, you know them best.

CASE STUDY

From Parents Deciding on the Best Early Years for Their Child

Ayesha and Lincoln needed to decide on where and what sort of early years setting to send their second child Gracelyn to. Gracelyn had multiple needs including challenging behaviour due to her sensory processing, delayed speech development, and she was on the pathway awaiting an assessment for Autism.

Ayesha and Lincoln had been managing well at home with the support of their health visitor who had put in further support for the family through a local multi-agency team. They had support from a caseworker who visited them and gave them advice on managing her behaviour and had recently been referred to speech and language support and to the paediatrician.

Their first child had attended a local nursery as Lincoln worked long hours and Ayesha returned to work when their first child was 2 years old. However, Ayesha and Lincoln were considering whether this would be the best support for Gracelyn, as they had concerns about how she would settle in and be supported.

Due to Gracelyn's needs, Ayesha had delayed going back to work, and had stayed with her until now, with Gracelyn aged 3 years old. But now Ayesha needed to return to work, although they were considering a part-time return to support Gracelyn's transition to an early years' setting.

They thought about the nursery provision that had been ideal for their first child. They were looked after very well there, and they made good progress transitioning into school with no issues or challenges. But they were not convinced that this would be the right approach for Gracelyn. Ayesha and Lincoln were concerned that being left all day in a large setting may contribute to her feeling overwhelmed and exacerbate her challenging behaviour, and they thought that she may need a quieter environment. They also decided that maybe a pre-school attached to the school where their other child attended might be good, in preparation for the transition into school, and Gracelyn could see that her sibling also attended the school.

Due to the hours of the pre-school, Ayesha decided that initially she would return to work part-time while Gracelyn settled into pre-school, and then if she was able to settle in well, she might increase her hours and consider a family friend who was a childminder to support them with Gracelyn with the additional hours, as this person knew Gracelyn and her needs. They decided to take a flexible approach and to see how the transition progressed before making any decisions on additional hours.

FROM EY TO RECEPTION

Once your child is due to turn 5 years old, they will begin to start within a reception class that will be incorporated within a primary or infant school. You may decide that you would like your child to start in September after they are 4 years old, or you may want to delay this. This will depend upon how they have settled into their pre-school provision, what support is in place for transition, and whether you would like them to start in September with the rest of their cohort. There will be benefits to your child starting as soon as possible and getting settled in with their peers rather than starting later, but you may also decide that there are benefits to waiting if they are progressing well and are supported at pre-school, or if you would like them to continue part-time.

Delayed Entry

If your child was born between 1 April and 31 August, you may decide on a delayed entry to school for them. Instead of entering reception with the rest of their peers, they would start in Reception in the September following their fifth birthday. You would need to ask your LA if your child is able to do this, and they can refuse this.

Deferred Entry

This is when your child would have a delayed start to the year, but still be in the same year group as their peers. For example, they may start Reception at the start of the spring or summer term. However, the school does not have to hold their place open for your child, so you may risk losing this if another child moves into the area and you may not get the school of your choice.

Your child's school will liaise closely with your child's pre-school; they will be arranging transition visits, and you will be invited to these.

Professional Discussion

Consider what questions you would like to ask your child's new school when you visit. Will you be speaking with their class teacher? Are you able to meet with the SENCo?

You may want to ask questions such as:

+ How many times will my child visit before they start? Can additional visits be made if needed to support your child?
+ What strategies will they use to settle your child in?
+ Will your child start part-time or full-time in the beginning? Some schools will start them part-time for the first week or so.
+ If your child is not settling in, how will they communicate this with you?
+ If your child has a support plan in place within their pre-school, how and when will this be implemented and reviewed?

You may want to ask further specific questions relating to your child's needs such as:

◆ How is your child going to be supported with toileting needs?
◆ What equipment and resources will be used to support your child?
◆ How will TAs/LSAs be deployed in your child's class?

Add to this list any specific questions that you think that you may need to ask.

RECEPTION TO AN INFANT OR PRIMARY SCHOOL

Your child should progress from Reception into Year 1 within an infant school or primary school, which is normally the school that your child's Reception class is part of. The transition will be planned through visits, and your school SENCo will support this if needed.

Year 1 will be more structured in the environment, and expectations will change for your child. Some schools will have Year 1 classes that begin by working in a way more like a reception class, making the transition easier while getting to know staff. For others, expectations will change from the start; your child may be expected to sit for longer periods of time for teacher input or for activities, they will have less time for "free play", and there may be expectations around lunchtimes.

Find out what that will look like for your child's transition, will additional support be needed as they move into Year 1?

The support in primary school can vary due to the size of the school; a smaller primary school may seem appealing for your child as it appears quieter and calmer, but a larger primary school may be able to distribute its funds more widely, with greater access to intervention programmes if your child needs them.

Infant to Junior

Some schools will be split into an infant and junior school. Most of the time, these split schools are on the same physical site, or very close by. Some infant and junior schools will work closely together and may even have the same governing body, others will work very separately.

If you are concerned with adding another transition point for your child, you may want to consider this when deciding on primary education for them.

PRIMARY TO SECONDARY SCHOOL

The primary to secondary school transition can sometimes feel like the most daunting when it arrives. You and your child will have become familiar with their primary school setting, the processes and procedures that are in place, and the staff that support your child.

Primary schools often support SEND pupils very well, they draw on resources across the school to support groups of pupils, and larger primary schools may have a very good number of interventions in place that can be accessed. Your child may feel safe and secure in their environment at this point, knowing key staff that understand them well after a long period of time working with them, and a move to a large secondary school can bring about anxiety and stress for both your child and yourselves as parents and carers.

Let's look back at the top tips from Maria:

TOP TIPS FROM MARIA

1. Ensure that you arrange visits at the local schools for your child, consider all of the schools, even if you have children already at a school. Think of them as individuals; one school may support your child differently than other schools and children.
2. Speak with a SENCo of the new school, and ask them for real examples of how your child might be supported.
3. If you are applying for an EHC plan, apply early for a transition, do not leave it until year 6, as things can take longer than expected, even when there are statutory responsibilities in place.
4. Keep an open mind to the different schools, do not listen to what others say, each school is different for each child, make your own visits and make your own mind up as to which school will be best for your child, remember, you know them best.

Consider this carefully when approaching this transition point, and what this transition will look like and mean for your child.

Your child's primary school and their connecting secondary school will be working together on transition for your child. This should start as early as possible. It may include early visits for discussions between the two school SENCOs, which will then be followed up by visits to the school for your child. This could start as early as January or February before your child moves to secondary school, but often this will start in the summer term after the school break.

Some secondary schools will arrange for a small group of pupils moving to their school to attend events that the school is hosting, such as performances or sports days, so that your child can gain an understanding of the wider experiences that they may be able to take part in when they have moved school.

Your child's visits should include meeting with teachers, familiarising themselves with key support staff, buildings and classrooms and how they move around them, and where to go if they have any problems. Visits may include taking photographs, creating maps or booklets of key information.

Professional Discussion

Ask both your child's primary SENCo and the key member of staff at the secondary school;

 ✦ What will transition look like for your child?
 ✦ When will this start?
 ✦ What activities will be put into place.

Think about whether there is anything else that you think would be useful for your child to support them with their transition. You will know them best and can contribute if you think there is an activity that might support them with a smooth transition.

Middle schools

Some schools in different LAs opted for a three-tier education system. This consists of:

 ✦ 5-8 age within primary, followed by 8-12 middle schools and 12-16 (or 18) secondary schools.
 ✦ 5-9 age within primary, followed by 9-13 in middle schools and 13-16 (or 18) in secondary schools.
 ✦ 5-10 age within primary, followed by 10-13 in middle schools and 13-16 (or 18) in secondary schools.

Many of the middle schools have now been phased out, but there are still a few located within certain LAs.

If you have a local three-tier system, consider the benefits and drawbacks to the system for your child. You may feel as though your child will benefit from not attending such a large secondary school initially, and having an extra transition point would be preferable. For others, you may decide that you think it would be better for your child to have just the primary to secondary transition point.

SECONDARY TO POST-16 OPTIONS

Education is compulsory for your child until they are aged 18 years old. There is a different option for post-16 education:

Sixth Form (Attached to a School or Separately as a College)

This type of provision normally offers A Levels, T Levels and BTEC courses. Often, they are attached as part of the main secondary school, but within a different area or space within the school. Pupils may be asked to wear a uniform, or they may be able to wear their own non-uniform clothes. They are often run like the main school and have a school "feel" to them.

College

This is normally a separate provision. Pupils may be able to sit A Levels, but often they normally have BTEC courses, practical courses including electrical course, building, textiles, and hair and beauty, for example, and offer opportunities to re-sit GCSEs. Pupils will normally attend in non-uniform, and the college may have a more "grown-up" and independent feel to it.

Apprenticeships

Apprenticeships are when your child will be at a college for approximately one day a week, and working with support in a workplace setting for the rest of the week. Your child will gain qualifications for doing this, and they will receive an apprenticeship wage. Apprenticeships can be difficult to find in areas that your child may be interested in, and there will be an application process and interview in which other candidates will also be applying for. See the further reading section of the chapter to access apprenticeships.

CASE STUDY

From a Parent Supporting Their Child in Their Decision for Post-16 Education

Rosa has just started her last year in secondary school. She has an EHC plan supporting her needs. She has a diagnosis of autism, sensory processing challenges, general anxiety and dyslexia. She has found secondary school difficult at times and needs support with changing classrooms, busy corridors, she doesn't attend assemblies, and spends time in the inclusion room at the start of the day, break and lunch times, and if she can't cope with the classroom (which is around once a week).

Rosa has been getting on with her work okay, and she is getting about average grades, or a bit below. But she works hard and enjoys the lessons. Recently she has

---

become very anxious about exams because she wants to do well, and this has led her to have anxiety attacks which have increased in frequency.

We are now thinking about the best place for her to go once she has reached 16 years old. Ideally, she would like to go to the college in the next town, where they do a lot of creative subjects. She would maybe like to take up textiles further and do something with dressmaking for example. But realistically we don't think she will cope with all the change, the large buildings and site that the college is on, and the busyness of it all. We also don't think she will cope with the travel to and from the college as she would need to get a bus or train, which she has never been able to do yet.

The local sixth form attached to the school, maybe doesn't offer her the type of subject that she would like to do, but the environment is familiar to her, she will know the staff, and we can support her to travel to and from sixth form. We do not know whether she will get the grades needed to get in; she may nearly get them, but we are worried about the stress involved, she may not even be able to sit the exams! With her EHC plan, we have discussed with her careers adviser that they would make exceptions regarding grades if need be, and therefore she would be able to go to the sixth form.

We have looked at apprenticeships too, but Rosa hasn't seen anything she likes in subject areas that she is interested in, and some are quite a distance from us too.

We have decided our next steps to support Rosa in making a decision are:

✦ To attend the open events at both the sixth form and the college with Rosa and discuss what it feels like to her.
✦ Talk with her teachers about the possible subjects she could take at sixth form that she might like to do, and whether she will cope with the level of them.
✦ Take a route to the college with Rosa and see how she feels.
✦ Speak with Rosa's career advisor about travel training, and hear about other children's experiences of this.
✦ Rosa to take part in experience events at both sixth form and the college.

When we have gathered some further feelings and thoughts from Rosa when she has experienced some of these, then I think that we will be in a better position to see what might be possible, and what definitely won't work.

SPECIAL SCHOOLS

If your child has an EHC plan and a special school has been named as their provision, your child may make a move from their mainstream school to the special school at any time. It may be that your child has an EHC plan in place from an early age while they are at pre-school and start in a reception class at the specialist provision.

Special schools normally cater for pupils aged 4 years old right through to either 16 or 18 years old. This is normally on one site, but it may be in stages in different buildings on the site. Transition can be well planned for at a special school from class to class, year to year, and phase to phase.

There may be fewer adjustments needed, for example, there may be fewer teachers teaching your child, they may have the same teacher teaching more than one subject, and they may not need to transition around the school for different lessons as they would do in a secondary school, teachers may come to them for more subjects instead.

BEYOND 18 YEARS OLD

When your child approaches the end of their formal education, this can also be a worrying time for you and for them. What next? How will they cope? We will look at this in more detail in Chapter 8.

Here are some options:

Further College Courses

Your child may have a particular interest that they would like to pursue through another course, and they may do this through another further education course at a college. There are often mature learners at colleges such as these, and it may be a way for your child to develop further skills in a particular area or to develop their confidence.

Apprenticeships

As in the previous section on post-16, your child could pursue an apprenticeship. There are different levels of apprenticeships, and your child may build on what they have already been doing through an apprenticeship or college course. It would support them into a workplace setting, and they may have further support mechanisms in place such as a mentor or SEND support from the LA.

Explore the links on apprenticeships at the end of the chapter and also look at your LA website for further information on the support that they may be able to offer your child.

University

You and your child may consider university. There may be a lot of discussion around the subject and the course that they would like to follow, entry requirements and location of the university.

You may decide that a university close to home would be more suitable so that you can support them if needed, and you may want to explore what SEND support is available for your child at each University that you visit.

Work

You and your child may decide at this point that they would like to enter the world of work. You can find out from your LA if there is further support with applications and interviews, if there are local businesses that offer additional support for employees with SEND, and if the job centre can offer further support.

You may need to think about whether full-time or part-time work might be the most suitable, and how your child will travel to and from their place of work. There may be support for travel training as mentioned previously in Chapter 5.

Benefit Support

Your child may not be able to cope with any of these options at this time, and you can support them to consider an application for the necessary benefits, such as PIP which is outlined in Chapter 5, and they may be entitled to claim other benefits such as universal credit and housing benefit.

Further discussion on independent and supported living is outlined in Chapter 8.

If your child has an EHC plan, this may stay in place until your child is 25 years old. Support could be implemented through the EHC plan for further education for your child. Seek further guidance from your LA on what this will look like. Your child may be allocated a young person's career adviser for pupils with an EHC plan that can support you and your child to find the next pathway for them.

CHAPTER SUMMARY

This chapter has focused on the transition points within education. It has looked at the different types of early years educational settings, and there were questions to consider asking when visiting different places for your own child.

Reference was made looking back on the *Top Tips* from Maria to think about how this could apply in relation to an early years setting, and there was a case study from Ayesha and Lincoln who were deciding on how best to support their daughter Gracelyn's introduction to an education setting.

The chapter progressed through the ages and phases through Reception and infant, junior, primary and middle schools, with questions to ask on a school visit. There was information on transitioning to a secondary school, an exploration of post-16 options and a case study from parents supporting their daughter through exploring choices of this next phase which can be quite daunting.

There was an overview of how special schools were different in their organisation of phases, often catering for children aged 4 right through to the age of 18 years. With a final look at educational options beyond the age of 18.

REFLECT

Think back on this chapter, how have your transition points been previously for you and your child? If you were going through these points again, would you do anything differently?

Consider the next transition point for your child:

✦ How will you plan ahead for this?
✦ Are there any visits you will need to make?
✦ Are there any meetings with professionals you would like to have? What questions would you ask?

GLOSSARY OF KEY TERMS

✦ Early Years Foundation Stage (EYFS) - The statutory framework for early years education. It sets the standards for the learning, development, and care of children from birth to 5 years. The guidance within the EYFS framework ensures that early years leaders, practitioners, teachers, teaching assistants, and childminders can effectively support and nurture the learning and development of children in their setting, from birth to 5 years of age.
✦ National Curriculum (NC) - The national curriculum is a set of subjects and standards used by primary and secondary schools so children learn the same things. It covers what subjects are taught and the standards children should reach in each subject.

FURTHER READING

✦ Applying for an Apprenticeship. https://www.apprenticeships.gov.uk/apprentices /applying-apprenticeship# and https://www.gov.uk/become-apprentice/apply-for -an-apprenticeship
✦ Childminding UK. https://childmindinguk.com/parents
✦ Early Years Alliance. https://www.eyalliance.org.uk/how-choose-right-childcare -and-early-education

CHAPTER 7

HOW TO GET THE MOST FROM PARENTS' EVENINGS, REVIEW MEETINGS AND ANNUAL REVIEWS

CHAPTER AIMS

◆ To gain an understanding of the different types of engagement that you will have with your child's school through a range of meetings and contact points.
◆ To consider your role in these meetings, and how to prepare for them.
◆ To know about the different routes to take if things don't go to plan or as you would like them to for your child.

INTRODUCTION

This chapter will look at the different types of contact points that you will have with your child's school. Each section will consider the contact point such as a meeting, the purpose of it and what you might want to get from this for your child. There will be a focus on clear communication, celebrating your child's achievements, and supporting your child's next steps. There will be case studies demonstrating some of the difficulties and challenges that parents have faced, and how they have overcome these.

DOI: 10.4324/9781032689159-10

GENERAL CONTACT POINTS WITH YOUR CHILD'S SCHOOL

There will be many occasions where you have informal contact points with your child's school. This could be when you are dropping off your child or collecting them at an early year's provision or primary school. You might take the opportunity to check in with your child's class teacher, seeing how they are getting on, whether there have been any challenges, or if there has been something to celebrate. This is a good opportunity to keep contact open with them and to know how things are going on a daily basis.

Some schools, however, would prefer a direct appointment to be made if you have any concerns or would like to discuss anything of concern. Teachers can be incredibly busy, and they don't finish work when your child leaves the classroom. They may have around three meetings to attend each week straight after school for whole school meetings, group planning and preparation, and assessment. They will also have lots of jobs to do such as marking, planning and assessment. Therefore, to plan a time in to speak with your child's class teacher can be better for both the teacher, who can set aside this time and plan ahead for it, and for you and your child so that you are not rushed and the teacher can give you their time to explore what your concerns may be. Find out what approach your child's school and teacher take, so that you know how to approach them when you want to discuss something.

In secondary school it can be quite different as you may be dropping your child off at the school gate, support hub, or they may be travelling alone or with friends to school. Often your contact will be by telephone or email, and it may be to check on something that is needed, such as a school trip, homework or an incident. As your child is with many teachers each week, it can be trickier to have open contact than it is in primary school, and you may want to establish a contact person to discuss your worries or concerns with, or just to check in with someone. This might be your child's form tutor, a SENCo, one of the SEND team, a year group leader or pastoral leader. It makes things easier when you have a contact point as the case study demonstrates below.

CASE STUDY

From a Parent with a Child at Secondary School

Henri is an anxious child, and he struggled a little with his transition to secondary school. He wanted to make sure he got everything right all of the time, and he would become very worried if he wasn't sure of something, or if there was a change in school that he didn't understand. For example, when he and his class were due to go on a school rewards trip, he wasn't sure if they were wearing uniform or not, and although a letter had come out, he had heard different things from his peers and he was confused. He became stressed about this saying that he didn't want to go as he might wear the wrong things.

As I have established a good contact with the SENCo and the inclusion hub manager over the last year, I was able to email them straight away and ask for them to confirm what the arrangements were. They were able to confirm the arrangements by email so that Henri could read this, and because it was from them, he knew he could trust what they were saying. He was then able to relax and enjoy his reward trip, while wearing his own clothes.

There are many contact points like this with the inclusion manager that we have. I try not to pester them or go to them with everything, as I know they are really busy, and they are working with many children, not just Henri. But when Henri is feeling anxious about something, and I know that a little bit of clear communication from someone in school is reassuring to him, then I just send a quick email so that he can have that confirmation. I always make sure I am polite and positive, as I know that they are managing a lot of work, and I can add to this sometimes!

PARENTS' EVENINGS

Traditionally known as parents' evenings, some schools now hold these during the day on what is classed as an INSET training day. These may then run over the course of the day and evening.

Parents' evenings have a different purpose depending on what school your child is in, so read any information given to you by the school in preparation for the meeting. For example, the meeting could be held in which you would sit and look through your child's work, and your child's class teacher/s would talk through what they are doing well, what isn't going so well, and what grades your child is getting. Other schools will choose a different approach, and you may not know what grades your child is at via a parents' meeting, but instead the focus will be on next steps for your child. Grades may be communicated to you on a termly basis, or in an end of year report instead.

Pupils may also gain grades for other areas outside of their academic achievement including behaviour, motivation and engagement in lessons. Some schools will encourage pupils to attend these meetings to keep open communication so that your child can hear what is being said, and any targets can be discussed with them at this meeting.

Parents' meetings may be face to face, online or you may be able to choose. Sometimes they are held in classrooms, and others in noisy halls.

ACTIVITY

In preparation for your child's parents' meeting, think about, and find out the following:

- What is the purpose of the meeting? Is it to share work, talk about next steps, share grades or celebrate achievement? Or a combination?
- Will you have the opportunity to discuss any concerns that you have? Or will a separate meeting need to be arranged for this?
- Will your child be attending? If so, are there things that you would rather not discuss in front of them? Can these be discussed at another time?
- If you are in a secondary school and moving from teacher to teacher, how will your child cope with this? Would it be better to join online if this is an option, or to arrange meetings at another time?

Usually at a parents' evening meeting, any support plans, IEPs and EHC plans will not be discussed in this meeting. These will be discussed at the relevant review points which are outlined in the next sections.

In some schools, parents' evenings are also the opportunity to look at what work is happening in your child's classes, displays will show the work being covered, and some classes or subjects may put on demonstrations such as languages, or being able to do food tasting or crafting. Take this opportunity to get to know your child's school and engage in discussion with them around these activities if you are able to attend.

The standard format for a parents' evening is:

The class teacher will:

- Start with a summary of your child.
- Talk about their strengths and progress.
- Talk with you about your child's areas for development and next step targets.
- The teacher may then talk about actions that they will take to support your child to take the next steps.
- Take feedback from you and note this down.

You may be limited to around ten minutes within a primary school, and it may be less, at around 5-7 minutes per subject within a secondary school.

TOP TIPS

For Parents Evening

- Don't save up any big issues for parent's evening as there isn't enough time. Speak to your child's teacher straight away so that you can work together to address any problems.
- Plan the questions you want to ask in advance, write them down and take them with you so that you don't get pulled off track in the moment and forget to ask them.
- Teacher's will want to be open and honest with you. But working with parent's can be challenging for them, particularly for newly qualified teachers. Set them at ease by saying that you really value their honest opinion of how your child is getting on and you want to help support with their learning.
- Read through your child's latest school report to remind yourself of where the school feel their strengths and challenges are, and where they were at last time you had feedback, then ask your child if there's anything they'd like you to discuss with their teachers on their behalf.
- Ask for another meeting if you don't get through what you'd hoped. Getting the best from your child's education is an ongoing partnership between you, your child and their school.

Professional Discussion

With the Class Teacher/s During a Parents' Evening Meeting General Questions to Ask

For parents of primary and secondary school children:

- What can I do at home to support their learning?
- Is my child doing the things you'd expect at their age?
- What do you feel my child's strengths are?
- Are there any areas where my child needs some extra help?
- Is there anything that has really worked to get my child engaged in their learning at school?
- Does my child seem happy at school? Have they made friends?
- Is there anything that is causing you concern as their teacher?

Parents of secondary school children could consider these questions as well as the above:

- Is my child on target to get the grades they are capable of and is there anything we can do at home to help?
- What opportunities has my child been given around planning for their future career?

These are more general questions, and some of them may be answered already in review meetings, in which case you could focus on taking the opportunity to enjoy your child and their teacher sharing their work with you, and updating you on how they are doing since you last met with them.

Are there any specific questions that you would want to ask your child's class teacher that you could add?

REVIEW MEETINGS

One-plans, IEPs and termly EHC plan reviews are all regular types of review meetings. These meetings happen in addition to parent's evenings, and normally happen around every term. There is a requirement that parents are given feedback at least once a year, but in most schools, this will happen termly to keep track of your child's progress against their targets, and to ensure that clear communication is happening.

The termly review may either be with your child's class teacher, assistant SENCo, or SENCo depending on how your child's school is structured.

Often the termly review will be with yourself, and key professionals if they are involved in supporting your child, might be invited, or they may send a report or an update of your child's progress. Your child will have some input into the meeting, their voice will be heard through contributing either in person, or through working with an LSA or TA to write down their comments against a contribution form or template.

There are *Top Tips* after the section on professional and multi-agency meetings (coming up in the chapter) which will be useful to use within these meetings too, but often these meetings are more relaxed as there are fewer of you, and you may feel more comfortable asking questions.

CASE STUDY

From a Parent

It can be really difficult as a parent of a child with SEND. There are many things we are getting used to, and we have lots of worries and questions. For example, how do I get support for my child? Will they make progress? What does the future hold for them? It can be a really worrying time, and some of the questions and fears are "big" ones that I don't have the answers to yet, but they can overshadow the day-to-day stuff. I have had some good relationships with schools and teachers, and other times not so good.

What has worked well has been;

* Being told by the teacher all of the good things that happen! Instead of focusing on the negatives, to hear what my child is doing well, on a daily or weekly basis means we can build on this. Instead of a phone call home to say my child is struggling and has had a bad day, to hear the good things really helps with having a positive evening at home and starting the following day in a good way.
* Keeping communication open so we can share things that are working well and not working, and being able to talk with a teacher when needed.

Things that haven't worked so well;

* Only hearing how awful your child has been.
* Not being able to talk with the teacher as they are too busy.
* I struggle when the teacher does not explain what strategies they are using, or they use ones that your child feels stressed about.
* Occasionally paperwork has not been completed correctly, so it holds up applications to services and has also caused me some difficulties with my child. I know everyone is busy, but my child comes first for me, and sometimes I expect this from others too and it makes me irritated when it doesn't happen!

TOP TIPS

From the Parent in the Case Study

From a parental perspective there are some good tips when making connections with teachers:

- Keep communication open, talk with your child's class teacher with any concerns and worries that you or your child has. The earlier you can start communication around a concern or issue, the earlier it can be resolved or sorted before it escalates.
- Remember to focus on the positives and not just the negatives. What is going well in school for your child? You may need to discuss challenges, but also include remembering to balance this out with the positives, it is important that your child is not just seen for the challenges that they have, and that they are regularly given the positives of what is going well for them.
- Work with your teachers to explain what works well for your child at home too. Implementing strategies across school and home can improve consistency. Although this may not always be the case, for example, some children may be more relaxed at home with less sensory demand on them and therefore behave differently. Other children may prefer the routine and rules at school which provide a source of comfort and safety and have challenging behaviour when they return home. Or, they bottle all of their stresses throughout the day and let them overspill and explode when they reach the comfort and security of their own home. Consider these differences and talk them through with your teacher. Is there any way you can support each other by identifying the differences in the environment, and in some ways replicate some of the things that are working well?
- In some cases, you as your child's parents or carers could be more educated and experienced than the class teacher in your child's needs. You may have been on training courses, or read up around the subject. In other cases, you may have less understanding around your child's needs in the classroom. Draw from each other and if needed, ask for support on where to seek advice and additional guidance.

It is important to note that teachers and SENCos should not contradict a diagnosis; this can cause tension with you as parents and carers. They are not trained to make a diagnosis, and your child will have undergone a rigorous assessment procedure. The strategies of support that will be put in place for your child in school will be in relation to what they are presenting in school, and this should be the same regardless of whether your child has a diagnosis or not.

EHC PLAN ANNUAL REVIEWS

There is a requirement that all pupils with an EHC plan are to have their plan reviewed formally at least every year. This is specifically referred to as the Annual Review. As seen in a previous section, most schools will be reviewing targets and progress towards these much more regularly, normally once a term, but this review is the formal review of the plan, when the evidence towards progress made is discussed and new targets may be set.

If your child is in early years, their EHC plan should be reviewed every three to six months instead.

This annual review is the statutory process of looking at the areas within the EHC plan, focusing on the needs, provision and outcomes that are specified within it. A discussion will take place around whether your child has progressed towards these targets, by how much, and whether any of these targets need to stay the same, or now be changed. It might be that your child has other areas of need that have become prevalent in the last year, or something else has become a challenge for them.

What the process of the review will look like:

- First, the LA must consult with you and your child's school about the EHC plan, and seek your views on how things are going and your wishes and feelings.
- A meeting must take place to discuss the plan and any changes that might take place.
- Information will be gathered from professionals working with your child, and this information should be circulated two weeks before the review meeting.
- Once the meeting has taken place, a report of what has taken place should be sent to everyone that has contributed, for example yourself as parents and carers, the school, and any professionals that have sent information in.
- After the meeting has taken place, the LA will review the plan, making any changes needed, and will notify you of the reviewed plan, which you will receive a copy of within four weeks of the meeting.

These steps must be followed in order for an annual review to be completed. However, with LAs being understaffed, you will often find that the LA does not attend the meeting themselves at all. It might be that your child's SENCo calls the meeting, discusses your views at the meeting, discusses the input and feedback from class teachers and professionals, and amends the plan according to your child's needs. They will send this off to the LA to officially amend and approve.

You should be happy with the decisions around your child's education and support that have been made in their annual review. If you are not, and the LA has not followed the process correctly, then you will need to escalate this through the LA complaints procedure that was outlined earlier in Chapter 5.

PROFESSIONAL AND MULTI-AGENCY MEETINGS

Your child may have multi-agency meetings throughout the year to enable a group of professionals to get together around a table and discuss their progress in a range of areas. These meetings may be in addition to a review or EHC plan meeting, and will give the professionals the opportunity to explore areas of support for your child and for the family as a whole. You will be invited to these meetings, and they can be very daunting sitting in a room full of professionals all discussing your child and your family. The next section will look at the range of professionals possibly involved with working with you and your child, and following this will be some tips for dealing with this type of meeting.

Educational Professionals

There may be many different professionals working with your child, either within school, or outside of school. Each of these professionals may contribute to EHC plan annual reviews, or professional or multi-agency meetings. Outlined below are some of the key professionals that may be working with you and your child:

- Behaviour Support Advisers – These are advisers that will come into schools and support with strategies for teachers to implement.
- Behaviour Support Home Workers – These workers work closely with Behaviour Support Advisers, and they work with parents and carers in the home to join up the thinking around the strategies and support in home and school.
- CAMHS team – The mental health team may work with your child regarding support for mental health concerns or anxiety. They may have group sessions or individual sessions, and these may be over an allotted period of time, for example 6–8 sessions. Progress would then be monitored and feedback given to yourself and the school.
- Education Welfare Officer (EWO) – An education welfare officer is responsible for monitoring attendance at school. If your child is having difficulty attending school, maybe due to high levels of anxiety, then an EWO may be involved in supporting you and your child to increase their attendance and they may attend multi-agency meetings. The EWO also supports the school when attendance is low and fines may be given to parents of low-attending pupils.
- Educational Psychologist (EP) – The EP may be involved in assessing your child; they might conduct tests and assessments to provide a picture of the areas of difficulties for them. The EP role is understaffed, and it can be difficult for all pupils who need to be seen by an EP to be seen quickly within a school. If a pupil has been put forward for an EHC plan and the assessment is taking place, then an EP will conduct assessments and write a report for this.
- Family Liaison Officers – These are part of a multi-agency team and may work with families on a particular area of need of the family.
- Physiotherapist – A psychotherpist may work with your child on movement and body functions to improve health and well-being.
- School Mental Health Team – Within the school, there may be an allocated Mental Health Practitioner such as MIND Mental Health charity or Well-being and Resilience Mental Health Service (WARMS).
- Social Worker – A child or family may be under the care or support of a social worker who will monitor safeguarding the child.
- Specialist Teachers – These will be within a certain area for example autism, neurological, or hearing or visual impairments. They will come into school and work

on a one-to-one basis with your child to develop particular areas of need from an action plan from their IEP or EHC plan.

✦ Speech and Language Therapists – Your child may attend sessions outside of school, or within school, working on areas of development.

✦ Virtual Headteacher – This is a headteacher that oversees all of the Looked After Children (LAC) that are in care in their Local Authority (LA).

As you will see from the list above, there are many professionals that may be involved with supporting and working with your child. Some of these roles may have slightly different titles or roles depending upon which Local Authority (LA) you work in, and how the LA has developed these roles. You may have come across other roles too that are not listed above.

If there are multiple agencies working with a pupil, then regular multi-agency meetings will be held to discuss areas of progress for the child and continued areas of support.

In addition to the education professional roles, your child may also be working with medical professionals too.

Medical Professionals

There are a range of medical professionals that your child may also be working with. These include:

✦ CAMHS mental health support – As outlined above.

✦ Consultant – Your child may have been referred to a specific consultant for assessment or tests of a specific nature.

✦ General Practitioner (GP) – Your child's GP may be referring to other services, or for further assessment of needs. They may be issuing medication for mental health, or co-existing difficulties such as anxiety.

✦ Nurse – A nurse may be monitoring or reviewing your child for co-existing medical needs such as epilepsy or mental health.

✦ Occupational Therapist (OT) – OTs offer practical support for physical and cognitive barriers to learning.

✦ Paediatrician – Your child may be seeing a paediatrician for assessment, monitoring or review.

Reports from medical practitioners may be presented at a multi-agency meeting to form part of the overall picture of provision and support for your child.

> **REFLECT**
>
> What education professionals have you worked with throughout your child's time in education so far? What other professionals might you need to work with in the future? What role do they play in supporting your child?

TOP TIPS

Sitting in on multi-agency meetings can be a daunting experience. Have a look at the tips below and feel more prepared to gain the best out of this type of meeting.

- When invited to the meeting, check that you are available and that you are able to stay for the whole meeting; you do not want to feel rushed or need to leave the meeting.
- Reply to any invite so that the person chairing the meeting knows that you will be attending, and they will ensure that you have any paperwork beforehand.
- Let the chair know if you have any access requirements, for example if you need paperwork printed in a larger font, or have particular requirements if you are expected to be sitting for a long period of time.
- If you would like someone to attend this meeting with you for support, check with the chair of the meeting whether you are able to do this, and if so, confirm with them who will be attending.
- When you receive paperwork for the meeting, it will include an agenda so that you can see what to expect and in what order, this will help you to plan for conversations that may be coming up.
- You may receive further paperwork including reports from professionals and specialists. Make sure you have received these in plenty of time to read through them and to understand them as far as possible. Write notes on reports if you would like to seek clarification of anything that is written, is there something that you don't understand? This is fine and normal! The person writing them is working in a specialist field, and you are not expected to understand their terminology or acronyms.
- Write down any questions that you have, and take a notebook in with you, so you can write down responses; you won't remember everything by the time that you get home!
- Check with the chairperson whether they would like you to send in any questions and clarification before the meeting, or to ask them at the meeting. Sometimes, if something needs clarifying on a report, it can be easily done beforehand, or, for example, a short pre-meet with the SENCo to explain, and you may feel more confident going into the meeting.
- When you are in the meeting, you should be given the opportunity to contribute and ask your questions. The chairperson should manage this by including you and checking in with you if you have any questions. However, if they do not do this, then do raise your hand, ensure that the chairperson or professional talking notices this, raise it high enough to be seen, and then someone should invite you to speak.
- Ensure that you give the professionals time to talk and present their discussion in full; they may answer questions that you have already noted down.
- Find out who you need to contact if you have further questions after the meeting, often you can walk away, and after you have had time to reflect and process information, you may have generated further questions.

CHAPTER SUMMARY

Chapter 7 has focused on supporting you to understand the different types of meetings, contacts and school engagement that will take place around your child. It started by looking at general contact points, through casual interactions such as school drop-offs and collection times, and calling in to the school. It highlighted the importance of establishing a contact person, particularly if your child is in a secondary school, as this can head off anxieties that could increase, but can also be solved with clarification.

The chapter progressed to explore the different types of formal meetings such as parents' evenings, review meetings, EHC plan annual reviews and multi-agency meetings. The roles of a range of different professionals were outlined.

The chapter has included a range of *Top Tips* and questions throughout to draw upon when planning for your child's next meeting.

REFLECT

Think back on this chapter, what is the next meeting that you will have coming up for your child? How will you prepare for this? Are there any particular questions that you will want to ask, or any ways in how you will change the way you engage in a meeting?

FURTHER READING

- ✦ Education Endowment Foundation (2018). Working with Parents to Support Children's Learning. https://educationendowmentfoundation.org.uk/education-evidence/guidance-reports/supporting-parents
- ✦ SEN Support and School Meetings – Useful Preparation Template. https://www.family-action.org.uk/content/uploads/2020/06/SEN_Support_and_school_meetings-1.pdf

CHAPTER 8

SUPPORTING YOUR CHILD AT HOME WITH THEIR EDUCATION

CHAPTER AIMS

✦ To gain an understanding of how to support your child at home with their education.

INTRODUCTION

This chapter will draw upon the voice of the parent. It starts with an outline of how children learn in school, and then an overview of examples of support for your child, and how you as a parent can support your child at home with their learning.

SUPPORTING YOUR CHILD AT HOME WITH THEIR EDUCATION

Supporting your child at home with their education can be daunting, frustrating, confusing and exhausting. You are not a qualified teacher, you haven't been trained in strategies to teach your child concepts or to develop an understanding of how they learn.

This section is going to give you an outline of how your child will be taught and learn at school, which you can then draw upon and use consistent approaches to try that your child will be familiar with.

Let's start with an overview of how children learn.

DOI: 10.4324/9781032689159-11

Memory

There are three main types of memory that we all use all of the time. You may be more familiar with the second and third: working memory and long-term memory. However, the first, sensory memory, is less heard of, but it is incredibly important and even more so with our SEND or neurodivergent children.

First, for example, we see, hear, smell, taste or touch something (sensory), which is then drawn into our working memory, and we decide whether it is worth taking note of and committing our attention to it, and if not, then we discard it. As it works through our working memory, parts of that information are stored into our long-term memory.

When the sensory memory is activated, neurotypical learners will be able to filter out the information that they do not need to pay attention to, for example, a dripping tap, a ticking clock, the chatter of other children's voices or bright and colourful wall displays, but for some SEND and neurodivergent children, this type of stimuli becomes a distraction, and they cannot filter it out easily. Therefore, working memory is disrupted due to the oversensitivity of the sensory memory, with some children overloading their working memory with sensory information, causing sensory overload.

Once we have decided which stimuli to focus on, this then becomes part of our working memory. Then information which we want to hold on to is moved into long-term memory. Some of this is encoded, and some of this is lost. Retrieval practice is very important in strengthening recall from long-term memory so that we can use it again and again. Over time, recall becomes easier and the information becomes more easily accessible from our long-term memory if we recall it regularly.

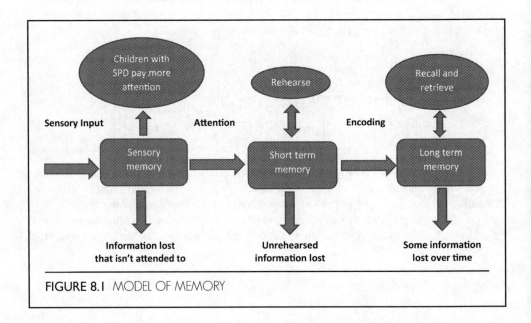

FIGURE 8.1 MODEL OF MEMORY

Model of Memory

The Education Endowment Foundation (EEF) (2021) *Cognitive Science Approaches in the Classroom; A Review of the Evidence* is a useful document which outlines effective learning theory approaches and strategies to use in the classroom, these are supported by evidence-based research.

Let's look at some of these now.

Metacognition and Self-Regulated Learning

When pupils think about their own learning, where they are at, what they are doing, and the choices that they make, this is metacognition: thinking about thinking. The EEF (2018) state that when the use of metacognition in the classroom is introduced and implemented effectively, then it can make as much as seven months' progress on children's learning.

Supporting SEND learners to take ownership of their learning to support their own progress, and to increase their self-esteem in knowing how to develop and adapt strategies to support their own learning, is very beneficial to them.

Sherrington and Caviglioli (2022) have written a set of books named *walk-thrus* to support teachers in the classroom. These give step-by-step guides to core teaching strategies for teachers to support their pupils in understanding the process and how to implement a particular strategy. This particular text outlines metacognition and self-regulation in five steps:

1. Explicitly teach how to plan, monitor and evaluate.
2. Model your own thinking (as the teacher).
3. Set an appropriate level of challenge.
4. Promote and develop metacognitive talk.
5. Explicitly teach how to organise and manage learning.

If you would like to take your support of learning to the next level at home, these books would be useful in explaining the strategies that are used in classrooms.

Cognitive Load Theory

Cognitive load theory centres around the use of working memory. Working memory can be overloaded, and I am sure that we can all think of times when we are trying to hold too much information and we forget things. This is because working memory has a limited capacity and when it becomes full, information will be lost. The Centre for Education Statistics and Evaluation (2017) discusses the theory of cognitive load. It outlines three types:

- ✦ Intrinsic load – In which if the complexity of the information being given is too high, and the underlying knowledge base of the learner has not reached this level yet, then the cognitive load for the learner is too much and the information will not be understood or retained. This has a negative impact on the learner.
- ✦ Extraneous load – This is when the learner is asked to solve a problem but they do not yet have the skills or the process to do this. The learner tries to the solve the problem, rather than use a technique that will help them to do this (think of maths problems and using formulae) because they do not have the formula. This will also have a negative impact on the learner.
- ✦ Germane load – This is when instruction is given to support the development of schema to then help learner progress. The instruction gives examples of how to work out the problem, and how it can be replicated when the learner is given a similar problem to solve. This will have a positive impact on learning. The use of modelling is a good example of this and is discussed later in this chapter.

Intrinsic and extraneous load can have a detrimental effect on SEND learners for both their learning and on their self-esteem when they find work overwhelming when they do not have the knowledge or skills to draw upon to carry out the task that has been given. This could potentially lead to negative behaviours being exhibited.

To reduce cognitive load, some SEND pupils may study fewer subjects in schools, for example, when they are choosing GCSEs or A Levels they may focus on certain subjects and spend more time on them to give opportunities to revisit content in their subject, rather than take on extra subjects.

Retrieval Practice

Retrieval practice can be seen in many lessons and is one of the more common learning theories that are understood and used by teachers. It is where the information is retrieved from long-term memory so that it is reinforced and is easier to retrieve the more that it is recalled. Retrieval practice is seen in the classroom through the use of quizzes and what is classed as low stakes questions or tests, in which pupils can retrieve the information without having the stress of formal exams or tests. It is often carried out in a fun and engaging way. It is good for self-esteem and when carried out in a safe environment it demonstrates that it is okay to make mistakes, or to not know something.

Spaced Practice

Spaced practice is when the teaching of concepts is taught over a prolonged period of time. For example, the content is chunked into sections and spaced out over a half term or term. It is often used alongside retrieval practice, and with content revisited back and forth.

The current focus in school is based around how children learn, and it is taken from what is called "evidence-based practice" or "evidence informed practice". As SEND parents, we also know that our children need to understand what they are learning and why they are learning it. Children may learn better through being active, and through social learning, and making connections between different learning and situations. This will be incorporated and entwined within classroom learning and is something that can be included at home.

High Quality Teaching (or Quality First Teaching)

High Quality Teaching is a range of strategies that are implemented in the classroom to ensure progress. Strategies include:

- ✦ Secure **subject knowledge** of the person delivering the lesson or teaching.
- ✦ Making **explicit links** between what your child already knows, and the new knowledge that is being introduced.
- ✦ The use of **small step planning** to support cognitive load (as discussed earlier) and working memory so that pupils do not have to cope with too much information, or information that they do not have the skills to work with. The use of chunking is useful here.
- ✦ **Planning for misconceptions** and errors that pupils may make. Anticipating problems will help teachers to be prepared to support pupils and recognise what may need to be changed.
- ✦ Using **manipulatives and resources** to support pupils through scaffolding learning and pupil understanding. Scaffolds such as physical resources and writing templates can be removed as pupils develop their skills and confidence.
- ✦ Using **metacognition** by the teacher LSA or TA when explaining will show pupils their own thinking process that they are going through, and the choices that they have made.
- ✦ Teaching explicitly **new vocabulary**, giving examples of how and when it might be used.

Modelling

Modelling is the clear demonstration of the steps used when teaching a method, for example, how to do a maths calculation, or how to write a sentence. The use of modelling is a key part to any lesson by a teacher, and they will use this repeatedly with their pupils if it is needed to ensure that they understand the method being used. Repeating the modelling, or using different examples support SEND pupils to embed the knowledge and skills from working memory to long-term memory is a key teaching strategy.

All of the above strategies and learning theories are used in the classroom. You could start to consider how they are used, and how you might change how you are supporting your child at home with their learning.

ACTIVITY

Choose one of the areas above, and practice using it with a piece of home learning that your child has. For example:

Modelling – Your child has brought home some maths sums to do.

1. Work through the first one on your own with your child watching, and talk through what you are doing and how you are doing it.
2. Work through the next sum together, talk through what might be the next step, see what your child can do, and do parts of it yourself.
3. Let your child do the following sum on their own.

If they are struggling, go back to step 1 and re-model the sum.

Or make explicit links with their prior learning (which helps with their recall).

Before you start an activity, ask them what they remember about doing something similar. Can they recall a previous lesson or activity that was like this? What did they do? How did they do it?

Reading

Many SEND pupils have difficulties with reading for different reasons. Your child's school will have particular strategies or interventions in place that they may like you to use, and this section provides some general strategies that you could try using at home with your child too.

- ◆ Read written instructions out loud to your child first.
- ◆ Ensure that you give your child enough time to read and process the information given.
- ◆ Present materials clearly and without clutter so that your child can access the information that they need.
- ◆ Discuss the meanings of words and check that your child understands them, provide context for them.
- ◆ Encourage your child to highlight words that are key important pieces of information for them to use; they can write notes or doodles next to them.
- ◆ Consider the use of software such as text reading pens.

Writing

There are different reasons for pupils having difficulty with writing. It could be the physical aspect of writing, it could be processing information that is needed before writing, or generating ideas to begin the writing process. Some strategies that could support your child with some of these aspects are:

✦ Ensure that your child has a pen or pencil grip if needed.

✦ Allow time for your child to talk through ideas first, or to practise their sentences.

✦ Provide sentence starters to scaffold your child in beginning their work.

✦ Ensure that you have provided enough time for your child to complete a written task.

✦ Become a scribe to capture the ideas and sentences from your child, rather than the stress being on the writing, take the time to capture their ideas.

Maths

Some SEND pupils may have specific difficulties with maths such as dyscalculia. This can also be seen across a range of other curriculum subjects in which maths is commonly used such as within science. Strategies to support some of these areas include:

✦ Practise using calendars and diaries.

✦ Using timelines of events.

✦ Using timetables for travel.

✦ Using timers for tasks.

✦ Using a range of concrete mathematical equipment both in maths and in other subjects when needed.

✦ Explain the use of equipment clearly.

All of these are really good activities to do with your child at home.

Independence and Organisation (Executive Functioning)

Some SEND and neurodivergent children will have a neuro-difference in organising, preparing and planning. They have challenges in these areas that do not fit a neurotypical view of how to do things and the expectations held around these areas to deal with school and everyday life. This area of difficulty is known as a difficulty with executive functioning.

Within school, the challenges may be seen through your child not having the right equipment for the lesson, or they arrive at the wrong classroom at the wrong time. This is because their "executive function" does not work in the same way as your neurotypical children, and your child with SEND may find it overwhelming to cope with these elements on their own. This is an area that neurodivergent children may find challenging throughout their lives, so preparing them with access to supporting strategies that will be useful for them to take forward into adulthood is beneficial to them.

Some strategies to support executive function could include:

✦ Equipment lists for each lesson printed on the inside of their book, or as a booklet to make sure they take the right equipment to school.

✦ Timetables which include a visual element.
✦ Tasks broken down into small chunks.
✦ Time to check preparation against plans.
✦ Lists that can be checked off when something is complete.
✦ The use of alarms or reminders when something needs to be done.
✦ The use of organisational apps as reminders and timers (for example, Brain in Hand, Timmo). Apps such as these are really good to use at home as reminders when to clean teeth, or to prepare for bedtime, or what order to get ready in the morning.

Reasonable Adjustments

Schools will make reasonable adjustments for your child in school. It may be to access the learning in a different way, or to support sensory needs. An overview of some possible reasonable adjustments is given below, there may be some that would be appropriate to include when supporting your child at home too.

✦ Access arrangements to support exams
✦ Adjustment cards which allow your child to leave class early between lessons, go to the toilet, or to wear different items of uniform
✦ Ear defenders to reduce noise and distractions
✦ Emotional regulation resources, such as visual supports and emotional scales
✦ Fidget toys for your child to use when listening and concentrating
✦ Frequent staff check ins
✦ Key person in school
✦ Learning breaks added in
✦ Now and next boards so that your child knows what is coming up in their day
✦ Nurture pets, such as a therapy dog in school
✦ Quiet spaces or somewhere to take themselves to relax or regulate
✦ Reduced timetable
✦ Reduction in the number of subjects taken
✦ Sand timers so that your child knows how long they have on an activity
✦ Sensory resources
✦ Social stories to prepare them for an activity or change that is coming up
✦ Visual timetables and resources

General Additional Strategies for Supporting your Child with Learning at Home

Some further general strategies for supporting your child's learning at home are:

✦ Narrating - Talk about what you are doing and why you are doing something. Talk them through by narrating what you are doing. This will increase their vocabulary, and you can explain words that they may not know. This could be anything that you are doing, for example, cooking, cleaning or organising something.

✦ Thinking time – Make sure that you give your child "thinking time" when you ask them to do something, or if you are supporting them with a piece of work, present something, then give them some thinking time before expecting a response.

✦ Life skills – These are so vital when working with our SEND children, they can be anxious about using kitchen utensil and equipment, or they may need lots of reminders regarding self-care.

✦ Action recommendations from any reports – Ensure that you carefully read and understand any actions from any reports that your child receives. Are there any actions that you can implement at home?

✦ Follow their interests – Can you incorporate their interests into their learning?

CASE STUDY

From a Carer Supporting Their SEND Child with Homework

I found it really difficult supporting Matteo with his homework at first. Matteo came to live with us when he was 13 years old. He has ADHD and was struggling in school with his concentration and staying on track. I attended a meeting at the school to see if there was anything we could do at home to support him more, as I felt as though we wanted to do more, but I was unsure what the best way to approach it was. Matteo could be very unfocused, and if we tired to push him too much to sit down and do his homework, for example, it would normally end up in an argument and he would storm off and refuse to do it. I was finding it very challenging, but my husband was a little more relaxed about it, recognising that Matteo had a lot going on for him, and his self-esteem was quite low.

We knew he was capable of doing the work, it wasn't because it was too hard, but we also knew he didn't want to fail.

The meeting was really important as it gave us the "permission" from the teachers to take the pressure off everyone. We wanted Matteo to do well, as we know how important education is for Matteo's future, and we may have been applying too much pressure too soon.

His SENCo told us (in agreement with his teachers) that Matteo didn't need to approach the homework on his own. They said for us to do it for him, and talk through what we were doing and how we were approaching it. We then just put a note on it to say if we had completed it, or if Matteo had done any.

We started off by saying we were going to do it for him, and this was okay. Matteo laughed and said it would be too hard for us! Some of it definitely was! My husband and I would sit at the table and talk through it, then we would talk aloud about how we were going to start it, what would we do, what part to look at first, we would underline the important parts, and circle parts we didn't understand. Matteo would sit in the background watching something on his Ipad, but I knew he was listening in. If there was something we didn't understand we would throw him a question and he would help to answer it (we would make a note of this on his homework, as it showed his recall of something). Sometimes if he heard us doing something wrong and he knew the right way to do it, he would get frustrated and come and tell us what we should be doing.

We began to create an environment where learning was relaxed and fun, rather than pressured, and we all worked together. We got into the routine of all sitting at the table before dinner to "tackle" the homework, and if it was writing we would act as a scribe for Matteo, which he preferred.

It didn't always work, but most of the time Matteo was engaged in the tasks and demonstrated what he understood, but taking the pressure off him to do it all on his own at the same time.

TOP TIPS

How to Keep Them Engaged

Keeping children engaged in activities and learning can be a challenge! Here are some tips to support you with this:

◆ Give calm and clear expectations.
◆ Create visual prompts and a timetable for activities or for your day.
◆ Use technology to support engagement, such as computers, Ipads and gaming.
◆ Incorporate their special interests.
◆ Incorporate movement into activities.
◆ Make activities short lasting between 15-20 minutes.
◆ Make learning meaningful and relevant, explain why they are doing it, and how it relates to them.

REFLECT

Think about what might work to keep your own child engaged in home learning. Are there any particular subjects, interest or strategies that you feel would be important or effective in including?

It is also important to note that some children may struggle with learning at home when they relate home with relaxing, being a safe space to switch off from a potentially stressful day in school. They may need to retain this difference in settings. For children that need this clear distinction, work with your child's school to see if they can attend homework club before or after school to complete homework, would they be able to have some support during this time? Is it something that you could attend with them if they are still in primary school, for example, when you collect them, can you stay in the classroom with them for 20 minutes and listen to them read or practice their spellings before going home? Maintaining this clear distinction for your child could be really important, and it can form as part of an overall plan so that your child is not penalised for not handing in homework. Ensure that if this is something that would benefit your child, that you raise this with your child's SENCo.

CHAPTER SUMMARY

This chapter began by looking at how children learn in school, and reasonable adjustments that may be made for them. It then focused on looking at various forms of support for your child, bridging the gap between home and school, and understanding how your child learns at school and how you can support them with learning at home.

REFLECT

Think back on this chapter, how might you best support your child at home with their learning? What challenges do you anticipate will lay ahead? How might these change as your progress through the education phases?

GLOSSARY OF KEY TERMS

◈ Cognitive Load Theory – When working memory is overloaded, information is not transferred effectively to long-term memory.
◈ Executive Function – A set of cognitive skills that includes working memory, flexible thinking and self-control. These skills are used every day to learn, work and manage daily life. For neurodivergent children, executive function challenges can make it hard to focus, follow directions and handle emotions.
◈ High Quality Teaching – Where teaching methods are used to deliver high-quality teaching for all pupils.
◈ Metacognition – The process of thinking about learning.
◈ Retrieval Practice – When information is retrieved from long-term memory through the use of quizzes, questions and tests.

FURTHER READING

◈ Centre for Education Statistics and Evaluation (2017). *Cognitive Load Theory: Research that Teachers Really Need to Understand*. NSW Department of Education.

- ✦ Education Endowment Foundation (2021). *Cognitive Science Approaches in the Classroom; A Review of the Evidence.*
- ✦ Sherrington, T. and Caviglioli, O. (2020). *Teaching Walkthrus*. John Catt Publishing.
- ✦ Sherrington, T. and Caviglioli, O. (2022). *Teaching Walkthrus 3*. John Catt Publishing.

REFERENCES

Education Endowment Foundation (2018). Metacognition and Self-Regulated Learning. https://educationendowmentfoundation.org.uk/education-evidence/guidance-reports /metacognition

Education Endowment Foundation (2021). Cognitive Science Approaches in the Classroom; A Review of the Evidence.

CHAPTER 9

WHAT NEXT FOR YOUR CHILD?

LOOKING TO THE FUTURE

CHAPTER AIMS

✦   To discuss the next steps for you as a parent in considering support for your child as they progress beyond school.

INTRODUCTION

This chapter will draw upon the voice of the parent. An overview of examples of support for your child, and for you as a parent will be outlined, and then the chapter will be entwined with a number of case studies from parents discussing their own experiences, and how they have overcome these.

LOOKING TO THE FUTURE: SUPPORT BEYOND SCHOOL AGE

What happens when your child is due to leave education, whether that is at 18 years of age, 21 or somewhere in between? You will be having conversations around whether they will continue with further courses, be seeking employment, voluntary work or whether a work environment may not be suitable for them at this point in time.

DOI: 10.4324/9781032689159-12

You may also be deciding where your child will be living. They may be staying at home with you, or they may be wanting some independence, and they may need support with this. There are so many scenarios that they may be in, and all of them can be quite daunting for you all as a family.

You will need to assess what your child can cope with regarding employment, and seek support through an advisor. This might be through your LA if your child has an EHC plan, or it might be from a job centre or a charity. Explore what might work for them, what are their strengths and what are their worries? Is there support for them to enter the workplace?

It might be that your child is staying with you for many years to come, and you may need to see what benefits you are able to claim for to support their living situation, and costs and bills.

Your child may also have attended respite care over the years, staying away for a short period of time with another family or on a specialist holiday, for example, to give yourself a break as a carer. You may want this to continue.

Some young people may want more independence, and this could look differently for different young people. For example, your child may:

- Move into a supported living facility, with other young people with SEND.
- Move into housing on their own, with support from community services.
- Move into housing on their own with support from you as parents.

There is no right or wrong way to support your child's next steps, and it may be a bit of trial and error too. Your child may think that they want to be independent, but then find that they do not cope so well being on their own, or that they become lonely. This shouldn't be seen as a failure, but as an experience to see what works for them at this time. Their experience and skills will change over time, and supported living, or you supporting them to develop their independence at home with you might be a better option.

There are supported living services through the National Health Service (NHS), for example, for a person with a medical need such as epilepsy, or for someone with a disability or SEND. Further information and the link to this are in the further reading section of the chapter. Explore your LA "Local offer" too, and see what services and facilities are in your area.

Supported living housing can be:

- Shared houses, usually with two to four people living together with their own bedrooms and sharing a communal space. The bills would be shared equally.
- Single occupancy units, where people have their own property within a group of other single occupancy properties, and you would pay the bills individually as the tenant.

With both of the above, you would have communal support services included within the tenancy costs, or as an additional cost.

CASE STUDY

From Parents Considering Their Child's Next Step Towards Independent Living

I was terrified that Danya wouldn't cope with living on her own. Danya had said that she was really looking forward to having more space when she moved out and had her own place to live. She is autistic and she has high levels of anxiety. She had been really struggling at college, her attendance was quite poor and she was due to leave. As we moved into the summer, Danya was becoming more aggravated at home, showing mood swings and constantly asking for her own space. In a lot of ways, she was just like any normal teenager approaching their 20s. As parents, we discussed our worries, and we didn't think Danya was ready to move out, she didn't understand bills, she needed reminding of the simple normal things such as elements to care for herself, feed herself regularly and wash each day, we just didn't think she would be able to do it. She didn't cope in unfamiliar situations, what if someone knocked on her door and then she couldn't handle the situation. It was all quite worrying for us.

As Danya grew more insistent though, we knew that we had to come up with a solution, as it was putting more strain on us as a family. How could we support her in this transition and try and make a move successful for her? We spoke with the LA support worker who had been in contact with us throughout Danya's EHC plan, and explored our options. Danya didn't want to go into a supported group living arrangement, she wanted her own space to do what she wanted, when she wanted. But I was very hesitant to let her go far. We looked at rental places near us, and we found a small flat just in the next road to us. We wrote a big list of pros and cons, and decided that this was something we could try, it didn't matter if it didn't work, we were just around the corner. If Danya needed us, we could be there in two minutes, and we could support her when new situations cropped up that she couldn't deal with.

We made the move! Danya was excited to plan where her things would go, and how she wanted her place to look. I made her meals that she could warm up in the microwave, and three times a week I would go around and we could a meal from scratch together, something simple like making a big chilli or bolognaise so that some could be frozen. We created a shopping list on a board so that when anything was used up it could be added, and I taught her how to use the online shopping app, as she didn't like going to supermarkets.

I set her up on the Timmo app, and this reminded her when she needed to clean her teeth, go for a shower, etc., each day, and sometimes when she didn't feel like it, we would go around and remind her how important it was. It was okay to miss these things once in a while, but it was important for them to stay as part of her daily routine.

We made Saturday our cleaning day, that way it became a regular thing, the washing went on, the bathroom cleaned and the flat hoovered. We did this together for many months first, and then she began doing more and more on her own.

Danya needed a lot of support with her finances, and we set up two bank accounts, one for all her bills so that she knew how much money she would have for her own spending on food and other things. This was the most difficult thing as Danya loved to sit on gaming and spending on her games, which she needed to budget for. So, we opened a savings account for Christmas and birthday money that she could use for this.

I thought that Danya may get lonely, but I was surprised at how she was becoming more confident in herself, volunteering at the local library to gain skills in meeting other people in a workplace environment, and everyone was very supportive. When she went home, she enjoyed her time alone and on her gaming, and we saw her several times a week.

I am really proud of how far she has come, and how her independence is growing. We still have a long way to go, and I am certain that Danya will always need some support for dealing with her finances and self-care, or things may spiral quickly, but I can now see how she will be able to live semi-independently in the long term as long as she has a key person to turn to if needed and to keep an eye on her to support her to stay on track.

CHAPTER SUMMARY

This chapter has looked at potential concerns and worries as a parent, next steps moving beyond school age, and progression to potentially some form of independent living for your child. The case study in this final chapter has focused on the parental worry and concerns that you may have when reaching this stage in your own journey.

CONCLUSIONS

I wish you all the best with your personal journey. It may be tough along the way, but I am sure that it will be filled with precious moments and successes. Being a SEND parent is one of the toughest but most rewarding parts of my own life too. Seek support, seek guidance, and seek change.

FURTHER READING

- ✦ Supported Living Services. https://www.nhs.uk/conditions/social-care-and-support-guide/care-services-equipment-and-care-homes/supported-living-services/
- ✦ My family, your needs. https://www.myfamilyourneeds.co.uk/supporting-your-child/housing-options/

GLOSSARY OF KEY TERMS

Adaptive Teaching – Scaffolded support for pupils to achieve the same aims, goals and objectives as all pupils.

Advice and Support Services (IASS) – A service for parents of SEN pupils run by the LA. This service is provided free, it is impartial, and it is confidential.

Alternative Provision (AP) – Education that is based anywhere other than a school.

Code of Practice (CoP) – Statutory guidance to support pupils with SEND.

Cognitive Load Theory – When working memory is overloaded, information is not transferred effectively to long-term memory.

Early Years Foundation Stage (EYFS) – The statutory framework for early years education. It sets the standards for the learning, development, and care of children from birth to 5 years. The guidance within the EYFS framework ensures that early years leaders, practitioners, teachers, teaching assistants, and childminders can effectively support and nurture the learning and development of children in their setting, from birth to five years of age.

Education and Health Care Needs Assessment (EHC needs assessment/EHCNA) – An assessment undertaken by the Local Authority (LA) to decide whether an EHC plan should be issued.

Education and Health Care Plan (EHC plan) – A legal document for children and young people aged up to the age of 25 years who need more support than is available through special educational needs support. A legal document containing the provision that is set out for a pupil with SEND.

Executive Function – A set of cognitive skills that include working memory, flexible thinking, and self-control. These skills are used every day to learn, work, and manage daily life. Send or Neurodivergent children with executive function challenges can make it hard to focus, follow directions, and handle emotions.

Formative assessment – Formative assessment happens on a daily basis, and it forms part of your reviewing what you plan and teach your pupils.

The Graduated Approach – The cycle of assessment for SEND needs: assess–plan–do–review.

High Quality Teaching – The current term used in schools to represent high quality teaching available to all pupils, and that is ordinarily available.

Intersectionality – The interconnection of social categories, for example, class, ethnicity and gender, and the overlapping system of discrimination or disadvantage.

Learning Support Assistant (LSA) – An LSA will often work 1:1 with pupils, they may have a pastoral role, and support the implementation and conducting interventions.

Local Offer – The services and support that a Local Authority lists for potential access by families and schools for pupils with SEND.

Metacognition – The process of thinking about learning.

National Curriculum (NC) – The national curriculum is a set of subjects and standards used by primary and secondary schools so children learn the same things. It covers what subjects are taught and the standards children should reach in each subject.

Ofsted – The Office for Standards in Education, Children's Services and Skills – Ofsted is a government organisation. They report directly to parliament but they are independent of the Government, and, by law, they must inspect schools with the aim of providing information for parents and carers, as well as promoting improvement and holding schools to account.

Quality First Teaching – Quality First Teaching has been a popular term that has been used for several years within the education sector and by teaching staff. High-quality teaching that is differentiated and personalised.

Retrieval Practice – When information is retrieved from long-term memory through the use of quizzes, questions and tests.

Special Educational Needs Coordinator (SENCo) – Works within a school to coordinate the provision for pupils with SEND.

Summative assessment – Summative assessment is a formal assessment of a block of work which happens at the end of a period or block of teaching, such as at the end of a half term or term, or a particular topic or unit of work.

Teaching Assistant (TA) – A TA will tend to work across the whole class offering academic support to all pupils and being a good role model to them.

Note: Page numbers in *italics* indicate figures, and page numbers in **bold** indicate tables in the text.

access arrangements 51-54, 126

adaptive teaching 43; High Quality Teaching and 41; targeted **78**

Alix, S. 50

Alternative Provision (AP): academy/free school 12; arrangement 12; SEND and Alternative Provision (AP) Improvement Plan 5, **5**, 8-9, 17

annual review 69, 77, 113-114, 115, 118

apprenticeships 51, 102, 103-104

assessment: external professional 50; formative 40, 45, 47; Graduated Approach (*see* Graduated Approach); summative 40, 50-51, **52**; tools 49-50; types and purpose 40; *see also specific assessments*

assess-plan-do-review cycles 45-47, 69, 54; *see also* Graduated Approach

attention deficit hyperactivity disorder (ADHD) 7, 43, 50, 54, 65, 71, 127

autism 7, 11, 115; assessment 71, 97; diagnosis 14, 20, 28-29, 50, 65, 87, 102

Autism Diagnostic Observation Scheduled (ADOS) 50

banding 61, 76-77, **78-79**

behaviour interventions 31

behaviour support advisers 115

behaviour support home workers 115

British Dyslexia Association (BDA) 50

broad and balanced curriculum 10, 27

carers allowance 86-88; *see also* parents/ carers

Caviglioli, O. 121

Centre for Education Statistics and Evaluation 121

Chandrika, Devarakonda 16

charities 63-65, 70, 75, 88, 89, 115, 132

Child and Adolescent Mental Health Services (CAMHS) 29, 115, 116

childminders 95, 97

Children and Families Act (2014) **5**, 6

children's centres 95

classroom based interventions 32

class teacher 16, 21, 33, 35, 41; EHC needs assessment applying for 69-70; with families 27; feedback from 114; Graduated Approach of assess, plan, do and review using by 44-47, 54; with other professionals 28; parents and 27, 44, 108-110; primary 25; review meetings with 111; role and responsibilities of 20, 22, 26-29, 31, 58; secondary 34; working with Dario 28-29

Code of Practice (CoP) 4, 5, **5**, 11, 17, 19-20, 25, 41, 44, 76; behaviour interventions 31; classroom based interventions 32; class teacher, role and responsibilities of 26-29; collaborative interventions 32; development of 6-7; intervention programmes 31-34; learning support assistant, role and responsibilities of 30-31; metacognition and self-regulation interventions 33-34; one-to-one intervention 32; parent or carer, role and responsibilities of 34; peer tutoring 33; social, emotional and well-being interventions 32; special educational needs co-ordinator, roles and responsibilities of 20-25; teaching assistant, role and responsibilities of 30

Cognitive Abilities Tests (CATs) 45

cognitive load theory 121-122, 123

collaborative interventions 32

complex learning difficulties or disabilities (CLDD) 8

complex needs 7-8; *see also specific needs*

consultant 50, 116

contact points 107-109, 118; EHC plan annual reviews 69, 77, 113-114, 115, 118; parents' evenings 109-111, 118; professional and multi-agency meetings 114-117; review meetings 16, 27, 44, 48, 71, 111-113, 114, 118

Continuous Professional Development (CPD) 21

day nursery 94-95

deferred entry to reception 98

delayed entry to reception 98

Department for Education (DfE) 4, 9, 30, 41, 53

developmental language assessment 49

Disability Living Allowance (DLA) 65, 84-85, 89; care component 84; claiming 87-88; mobility component 84-85

discrimination 4, 16

dyscalculia 7, 125; assessment 49; screening tools for 45-46

dyslexia 7, 14, 102; assessment 49; diagnosis 50; screening tools for 45

Early Years (EY) 114; childminder 95; children's centres 95; considerations 95-96; day nursery 94-95; parents' decision on 97; pre-school 94; to reception 97-99; SENCo 21, 25, 32, 95-96; setting 20, 94-97, 105

Early Years Foundation Stage (EYFS) 51, **52**, 94-95

Early Years Foundation Stage Profile (EYFSP) 51

Education Act (1944) 4

educational professionals 16, 114-117; *see also specific professionals*

Educational Psychologists (EPs) 15, 22, 59, 60, 69, 71, 115

Education and Skills Funding Agency 76

Education Endowment Foundation (EEF) 30, 121

Education, Health and Care Needs Assessment (EHCNA) 9-10, 24, 28-29, 58, 63, 73-74; beyond 20 weeks 62, **62**; Local Authority and 24, 59-62, 67, 69, 114; parental experience of applying 59-62, 64-68, 80-81; people can apply 59; primary school pupil progressing to application 70-71; secondary school pupil

progressing to application 71-72; SENCo, applying for 59-60, 64-65, 68-70; steps involved 59-62; teacher, applying for 69-70; timeline **62**; time taken to happen 59-62; weeks 1-6, 59-60, **62**; weeks 6-12 60-61, **62**; weeks 13-16 61, **62**; weeks 17-20 61, **62**

Education, Health and Care plans (EHC plans) 3, 9-15, 21, 24, 27, 52-54, 57, 72-73, 110-111, 132; annual reviews 113-114, 115, 118; application 87, 100; applying as parent 67-68; benefit support and 105; choice on 82-83; defined 58-59; funding and banding 76-77, 80; implementing and reviewing 68-70; issues with getting right school 63-67; by Local Authority 58; needs for banding **78-79**; parent received and agreed to child's 80-81; purpose 63; special schools and 103; stages to 58; standard format 67; supporting needs 102-103; *see also* Education, Health and Care Needs Assessment

education other than at school (EOTAS) 13-15

Education Supervision Order 13

education welfare officer (EWO) 115

elective home education (EHE) 13

emotional intervention 32

emotional literacy assessment 29, 49

Employment and Support Allowance 85

English as an Additional Language (EAL) 51

Equality Act (2010) 4, **5**, 6

evidence-based practice 122

evidence informed practice 122

executive function 49, 125; strategies to support 125-126

external exclusion *see* suspension

extraneous load 122

family liaison officers 115

financial sustainability 8, 9

formative assessment 40, 45, 47

free play 99

funding 10, 14, 60, 63, 68, 72, 99; additional 61; being used to support child 80-81; carers allowance 86-88; charities 89; Disability Living Allowance 84-85, 87-88; EHC Plan 76-77, 80; High Needs Block funding 76-77; Individual Pupil Resourcing Agreement 81-82; lack of 61; Local Authority 12, 14, 76-77, 81-82; medical needs 82; Notional SEND Budget 76; personal budget 77; Personal Independence Payment

85-86, 87-88; Per Pupil Funding 76; to support transition 61; top-up funding 76-77; transition 61, 82, 87-88; transport 82-83; types 75-77

General Certificate of Secondary Education (GCSEs) 11, 15, 40, 50, 51, 53-54, 102, 122
General Practitioner (GP) 116
germane load 122
Government Department for Work and Pensions (DWP) 86
Graduated Approach 27-29, 41, 43, 44, 72; assessment stage 45-46, 54, 69; assess-plan-do-review cycles 45-47, 54, 69; do stage 47, 54, 69; model of 45; parents and 44-47; planning stage 46, 54, 69; pupil voice in 47-48; review stage 47, 54, 69; Special Educational Needs Coordinator and 44-47

High Needs Block funding see top-up funding
High Quality Teaching (HQT) 23, 27-28, 36n1, 47, 54; adaptive teaching and 41; home learning 123; model of 41-43, 42; strategies 123; Targeted Academic Support 41-42; universal support including 44; wider strategies 42-43
home learning 46, 64, 111-113, 115; action recommendations from reports 127; cognitive load theory 121-122; elective home education 13, 14; High Quality Teaching 123; homework, supporting 127-129; independence and organisation 125-126; life skills 127; maths 125; memory 120-121, 120; metacognition and self-regulated learning 121; modelling 123-124; narrating 126-127; reading 124; reasonable adjustments 10, 126, 129; retrieval practice 122; spaced practice 122-123; strategies 126-129; thinking time 127; writing 124-125

independence and organisation 8, 31, 81, 125, 132-134
Individual Education Plan (IEP) 24, 27, 46, 68, 69, 71
Individual Pupil Resourcing Agreement (IPRA) funding 81-82
Information, Advice and Support Services (IASS) 63, 65, 70
internal exclusion 72-73
intersectionality 16
intervention programmes 31-34; behaviour 31; classroom based 32; collaborative 32;

metacognition and self-regulation 33-34; one-to-one 32; peer tutoring 33; social, emotional and well-being 32
intrinsic load 122

Joint Council for Qualifications (JCQ) 53

Kozleski, E. B. 16

leadership team 23
Learning Support Assistant (LSA) 20, 23-26, 28-29, 34-35, 48-49, 64, 71, 112; metacognition by 123; one-to-one support by 30-32, 80; Teaching Assistant vs. 30; working with Dario 33
level 1 (or element 1) funding see Per Pupil Funding
level 2 (or element 2) funding see Notional SEND Budget
level 3 funding see top-up funding
Local Authority (LA) 20, 22, 63, 81, 95, 104-105, 116, 132; action 62; day nurseries by 94; Education, Health and Care Needs Assessment and 24, 59-62, 67, 69, 114; Education, Health and Care plan by 58; education other than at school and 13-14; expectations of 9-10, 17, 19; funding and 12, 14, 76-77, 81-82; home education and 13; lack of Educational Psychologist in 15; Pupil Referral Units and 12; roles and responsibilities of 3, 6, 17, 58, 70-73; special school placement and 11; three-tier education system and 101; transport cost and 82-83
Local Offer 10, 63, 70, 74, 83, 132
long-term health condition, defined 4
long-term memory 120, 122, 123

medical needs funding 82
medical professionals 116-117
memory: integration 49; long-term 120, 122, 123; model 120, 121; sensory 120; short-term 7; working 49, 120, 121, 123
mental health 8, 28, 44; assessment 50; CAMHS team 29, 115, 116; School Mental Health Team 115; support 25, 87
metacognition: and self-regulated learning 121-122; and self-regulation interventions 33-34; by teacher LSA/TA 123
modelling 123-124
moderate learning difficulties (MLD) 7, 14, 78
multi-agency meetings 114-117

national curriculum (NC) 94
National Health Service (NHS) 132

National Professional Qualification (NPQ) 20
National SENCo Award (NASENCo) 20
Notional SEN budget 76
Notional SEND Budget 76

Occupational Therapist (OT) 116
off-rolling 13
Ofsted (Office for Standards in Education, Children's Services and Skills) 94, 95; defined 21; descriptors 21
one-to-one intervention 32
one-to-one support 26, 30-31, 35, 47, **78**, 80, 89, 116

paediatrician 29, 50, 60, 71, 97, 116
parents/carers 8, 21-22, 26, 54, 59, 71-73, 100, 112-113, 131; best early years for child 97; with child at secondary school 108-109; child towards independent living 133-134; class teacher and 27, 44; complex needs, understanding of 7; contact points with school (see contact points); decision-making 17, 94, 97; Education, Health and Care Needs Assessment and 59-62, 64-68, 80-81; elective home education and 13; expectation about one-to-one person working 31; Graduated Approach and 44-47; grandparents 12, 84; Information, Advice and Support Services to 70; informing 6, 10; with Local Authority 24; paying transport 82; requesting fund 77; role and responsibilities of 34; seeking formal diagnosis 50; special schools and 11; step-parents 84; support beyond school age 131-134; supporting child in decision for post-16 education 102-103; support in home learning (see home learning); transitioning from claiming DLA to claiming PIP 87-88; trust 9; with year 6 pupil 14-15
parents' evening 109-111, 118; purpose 109; questions to ask 111; standard format 110
peer tutoring 33
permanent exclusion 13, 72, 73
Per Pupil Funding 76
personal budget 77
Personal Independence Payment (PIP) 65, 85-86, 89, 105; claiming 87-88; daily living part 85-86; mobility part 86
physiotherapist 11, 115
pre-school 94-95, 97-98
professional meetings 114-117

profound and multiple learning difficulty (PMLD) 8, **79**
protected characteristics 4
Pupil Referral Units (PRUs) 12-13

qualified teacher 20, 26, 110, 119
Qualified Teacher Status (QTS) 20, 95
Quality First Teaching (QTF) 23, 36n1, 123; see also High Quality Teaching

reading 28-29; assessment 45, 49, 51; difficulty with 51; home learning 124
reasonable adjustments 10, 126, 129
reasoning assessment 49
recall 53, 127-128; assessment 49; retrieval practice in 120, 122; strategies 28
Reception Baseline Assessment (RBA) 51
reception class 94, 103, 105; deferred entry 98; delayed entry 98; from Early Years to 97-99; to infant or primary school 99
refugee, with behavioural challenges 16
retrieval practice 120, 122
review meetings 16, 27, 44, 48, 71, 111-113, 114, 118

School Attendance Order 13
school mental health team 115
self-regulation: interventions 33-34; learning 121-122
SEN register 21, 43-44
sensory memory 120
severe learning difficulty or disability (SLD) 7-8, **79**
Sherrington, T. 121
Social, Emotional and Mental Health (SEMH) 13, 71
social, emotional and well-being interventions 32
social worker 60, 115
spaced practice 122-123
Special Educational Needs (SEN) 4, 6, 9, 12, 16, 26-28, 60, 63, 69, 82; assessment 73; health needs related to 67; Information, Advice and Support Services to parents 70; Notional SEN budget 76; register 21, 43-44; social care needs related to 67; Special Educational Needs Coordinator and 44
Special Educational Needs or Disability (SEND): alternative provision arrangement 12; categorisation of pupils 6; Code of Practice (see Code of Practice); complex learning difficulties or disabilities 8; and complex needs 7-8; defined 4; education other than at

school 13-15; elective home education 13; governor 21; inclusion and different settings 10-15; intersectionality 16; Local Authority, expectations of 9-10; moderate learning difficulties 7; National Standards for 9; policy and legislation relating to 4-5, **5**; profound and multiple learning difficulty 8; proposals of improving outcomes 8-9; Pupil Referral Units 12-13; SEND and Alternative Provision (AP) Improvement Plan 5, **5**, 8-9, 17; severe learning difficulty or disability 7-8; special schools 10-11; specific learning difficulties 7

Special Educational Needs and Disabilities Act (2001) **5**

Special Educational Needs and Disabilities Regulations (2014) 6

Special Educational Needs and Disability Tribunal (SENDIST) 60

Special Educational Needs Coordinator (SENCo) 4, 9, 10, 16, 20-21, 71-72, 80-81, 98-99, 113-114, 117, 127-129; assessment tools used by 49; assistant 43, 111; Deputy 32; discussions between 100; Early Years 21, 25, 32, 95-96; EHC needs assessment and 59-60, 64-65, 68-70; good contact with 108; Graduated Approach and 44-47; Key Stage 3, 32; Key Stage 4, 32; leadership team need to provide time to 23-24; primary 24-25, 32, 53, 101; qualifications of 20; as qualified teacher 20; responsibilities of 22-25; role of 21-22; secondary 25, 54; sort of activities 22; Special Educational Needs register and 44; strategic roles and tasks 23

specialist teachers 50, 69, 77, 115-116

special schools 7, 10-11, 14-15, 59, 103-104; drawbacks 11; positives 11

specific learning difficulties (SpLD) 7

speech and language therapists (SLT) 11, 25, 50, 69, 116

Standardised Assessment Tests (SATs) 40, 50, 51-53

summative assessment 40; process 50-51; stages and ages **52**

suspension 72, 73

Targeted Academic Support 41-42

teacher assessments 50-51

Teaching Assistant (TA) 11, 20, 23-26, 28, 34-35, 48, 112; Learning Support Assistant *vs.* 30; metacognition by 123; one-to-one support by 30-32, 80; role and responsibilities of 30-31

three-tier education system 101

top-up funding 76-77

transitioning 24-25, 29, 31, 64-65, 80, 133; beyond 18 years old 104-105; to apprenticeships 102, 104; to childminder 95; to children's centres 95; between classes 15; to college 102, 104; to day nursery 94-95; early years considerations 95-96; into Early Years setting 94-97; from Early Years to reception 97-99; funding 61, 82, 87-88; to middle schools 101; parents' decision on 97; to pre-school 94; primary to secondary school 100-101; reception to infant or primary school 99; to secondary school 15; secondary to post-16 education 101-103, 108; to sixth form 102; to special schools 103-104; to university 104-105; to work 105

transport funding 82-83, 87, 89; travel training 83; wider travel 83

travel training 83, 103, 105

trust 108; parent's 9

virtual headteacher 116

vocabulary: assessment 49; home learning 126-127; new 123

Waitoller, F. 16

well-being intervention 32

working memory 49, 120, 121, 123

writing 9, 53, 128; difficulty with 51, 64; home learning 124-125; targets 24-25; templates 123

Printed in the United States
by Baker & Taylor Publisher Services